PRAISE FOR LUKE MARSH

Crazy Random Facts for Car Rides is the perfect co-pilot—snappy, wildly fascinating, and guaranteed to turn every mile into a laugh.

— KAI MORENO, FAMILY TRAVEL YOUTUBER

From space oddities to food mysteries, this book makes quick reads feel like a mini road-trip show, sparking instant conversations.

— DR. ELENA PARK, EDUCATIONAL PSYCHOLOGIST

A must-have for any road trip—fast facts, big laughs, and zero data plan required.

— RAVI KAPOOR, TRIVIA NIGHT CHAMPION

CRAZY RANDOM FACTS FOR CAR RIDES

CRAZY RANDOM FACTS FOR CAR RIDES

A HILARIOUS COLLECTION OF WEIRD FACTS TO
MAKE ROAD TRIPS FLY BY

ROAD TRIP BRAIN BITES
BOOK ONE

LUKE MARSH

Copyright © 2026 by Luke Marsh

Published by Book Bound Studios

All rights reserved.

No part of this publication may be reproduced, distributed, or transmitted in any form or by any means, including photocopying, recording, or other electronic or mechanical methods, without the prior written permission of the publisher, except in the case of brief quotations embodied in critical reviews and certain other noncommercial uses permitted by copyright law.

Disclaimer: The information provided in this book is for educational and entertainment purposes only. The author and publisher make no representation or warranties with respect to the accuracy, applicability, fitness, or completeness of the contents of this book. The information contained in this book is strictly for educational purposes. Therefore, if you wish to apply ideas contained in this book, you are taking full responsibility for your actions.

The author and publisher disclaim any warranties (express or implied), merchantability, or fitness for any particular purpose. The author and publisher shall in no event be held liable to any party for any direct, indirect, punitive, special, incidental, or other consequential damages arising directly or indirectly from any use of this material, which is provided "as is," and without warranties.

First Edition

To the road travelers—the drivers who steer with patience, and the passengers who listen with wonder. To the backseat philosophers who turn every mile into a quest for odd, delightful truths. May these Crazy Random Facts for Car Rides entertain your commutes, spark your curiosity, and make the road feel a little less ordinary. For my family and friends who humored my obsession with trivia, and for every editor who believed this odd idea could keep you company on the highway—this book is for you.

Not all those who wander are lost.

— J. R. R. TOLKIEN

CONTENTS

Buckle Up for Brainy Giggles   xv

1. Animal Weirdos on Wheels   1
2. Space Stuff That'll Blow Your Mind   15
3. The Human Body's Funniest Glitches   27
4. History's Strangest Moments (Yes, Really)   41
5. Bizarre Inventions That Actually Existed   57
6. Food Facts That Feel Like Pranks   69
7. Earth Is a Weird Planet (Understatement)   85
8. Ocean Oddities (Even If You're Landlocked)   101
9. Bugs, Spiders, and Other Tiny Supervillains   117
10. Sports, Games, and Playground Trivia   127
11. Language, Words, and Silly Sayings   143
12. School Isn't Boring When the Facts Are This Weird   155
13. Technology and Internet Weirdness (No Wi-Fi Needed)   169
14. Famous People Did WHAT?!   181
15. Animals vs. Humans: Who Wins?   195
16. Gross Facts (But Not Too Gross)   209
17. Mystery Places and Hidden Wonders   219
18. Everyday Stuff You Never Noticed Is Actually Amazing   233
19. Quick Car-Ride Party Games Using Facts   247

Keep the Curiosity Rolling   261

BUCKLE UP FOR BRAINY GIGGLES

How to Use This Book: A Quick Guide

On a road, the car becomes a rolling wonder factory, and this book is your passenger seat guide. It's designed to feel like a quick jog through a park of oddities rather than a marathon through a textbook. Packed with bite-sized, clean, and curious facts—from space quirks to food mysteries—it invites everyone from six-year-olds to grandparents to join the ride. No Wi-Fi is required, just an open cover and a readiness to let laughter and learning ride side by side.

Think of these pages as a toolkit for interaction. You don't need to read cover-to-cover or set aside hours; you can jump in anywhere and still make a mile feel shorter. Whether you're on a quick pit stop or a long haul, the flow is flexible, allowing for short bursts of trivia or deeper dives into fascinating topics. It's an on-the-go mentor and a portable campfire designed to turn the car into a shared space for collaboration, where the aim is not to win a competition but to linger on moments of wonder.

Above all, the ride becomes a stage for curiosity. The content is crafted to be kid-friendly and accessible, breaking down big ideas into simple, clear terms that welcome questions rather than arguments. It's about connection—turning the drive into a memory-making moment where everyone gets to be the expert. The promise is simple: weird, true facts that are easy to share and impossible to forget. Welcome aboard, and let the brainy giggles begin.

* * *

Car-Ride Game Starters

Two Truths and a Fib - This is the engine of the backseat experience, transforming listening into friendly competition. A player uses facts they've just heard to create three statements: two real, one made up on the spot. It scales from a quick minute to a long stretch, rewarding recall and sparking laughter as everyone tries to spot the fib. It's playful, social, and requires nothing but your voices.

Guess the Topic - Swap competition for shared inference in this cooperative starter. One reader drops light, illustrative clues about a category—like animals or inventions—without naming it, while the car takes turns guessing. It's not about setting traps; it's about that satisfying nod when someone lands on the right answer. This approach gives everyone a chance to contribute where their strengths lie, making the ride warmer and smarter.

Rapid-Fire True or False - Kick up the energy with a round designed to celebrate the moment of surprise. A single fact is read aloud, and everyone shouts their verdict—true or false? The aim isn't to trap anyone but to spark a "No way!" reaction when a strange detail proves true. It keeps the whole car thinking on their feet, ready for a quick punchline or a raised eyebrow at the next turn.

1

ANIMAL WEIRDOS ON WHEELS

Invented-Looking Body Parts (That Are 100% Real)

If animals were designed by a committee of pranksters, some of these body parts would still sound too silly to approve. But nature doesn't care what sounds believable. It just keeps experimenting, and the results are hilarious, useful, and occasionally a little creepy.

A giraffe's tongue can be around 18 to 20 inches long, which is basically a travel-size scarf made of muscle. It's also often a dark bluish-purple. Scientists think the darker color may help protect it from sun exposure while the giraffe spends hours reaching into thorny trees for leaves. Imagine having a tongue that could grab your snack from the back seat without you even turning around.

Wombats come with one of the oddest rear-end features on Earth: a super-tough backside. Their rumps are reinforced with thick skin, cartilage, and bone, and they use them like a built-in shield. If a predator tries to chase a wombat into its burrow, the wombat can block the tunnel with its tough rear end, making it extremely hard for the attacker to get past. It's the animal version of slamming the door and saying, "Nope. Not today."

The narwhal takes "unbelievable" to the next level with what looks like a unicorn horn. That long spiral "horn" is actually a tooth, usually a canine tooth that grows out through the upper lip and can reach about 10 feet. For a long time people argued about what it was for, and researchers now think it can play roles in social behavior and sensing the environment. Yes, a tooth can be a fancy sensory tool, because animals apparently refused to read the rulebook.

Star-nosed moles look like they're wearing a tiny, wiggly sea anemone on their face. The "star" is made of 22 fleshy appendages packed with touch receptors. These moles live underground and in wet areas where vision isn't very helpful, so their star helps them rapidly identify food by touch. They're so fast at detecting and eating prey that it almost seems like a magic trick, except it's just a mole doing its weird little job.

Some frogs have toe pads that work like built-in climbing gear. Tree frogs, for example, can stick to leaves and smooth surfaces thanks to special structures on their toe pads that create grip using a mix of tiny surface patterns and moisture. It's not exactly glue, and it's not exactly suction, but it's enough to let them climb like they're auditioning for an action movie.

Chameleons are famous for changing color, but their eyes deserve their own spotlight. They can move their eyes independently, scanning two different directions at once. When they spot something interesting, both eyes can focus on the same target for a precise strike with that lightning-fast tongue. It's like having two separate windshield wipers that suddenly synchronize when a bug appears.

Octopuses don't just have eight arms; they have an absolutely wild nervous system. A large portion of an octopus's neurons are in its arms, not only in its central brain. That means each arm can do complex movements and respond to the environment in a semi-independent way. If your hands could "think" on their own during snack time, your car would be full of crumbs and chaos in about thirty seconds.

The blobfish became internet-famous for looking like a grumpy, squishy jelly when it's brought to the surface, but here's the twist: down in its natural deep-sea habitat, it doesn't look quite as dramatically blobby. The pressure at deep depths helps it keep a more normal shape. So the blobfish is basically a deep-ocean creature that gets unfairly judged for looking strange in the wrong environment, like someone taking your worst photo and making it your yearbook picture.

And then there are pangolins, which look like they're wearing overlapping armor made of scales. Those scales are made of keratin, the same material in human fingernails. When threatened, a pangolin can roll into a tight ball, presenting a spiky, armored surface that's hard for predators to deal with. It's like a living pinecone with legs, and it's one of the most "how is that real?" looks in the animal kingdom.

Next time someone in the car says, "That can't be true," you can calmly respond with the most satisfying phrase in trivia history: **It absolutely is.**

Gross-But-True Habits (Nature Has No Manners)

Animals do not worry about being polite. They don't care about "too much information." They're trying to survive, communicate, and occasionally impress each other, and if that involves slime, smells, or poop, so be it. The good news is you get to laugh about it from the comfort of a car seat.

Some animals eat their own poop on purpose, and yes, that's a real sentence. Rabbits, for example, produce special droppings called cecotropes that they re-eat to get more nutrients. Their digestive system needs a second pass to fully absorb certain vitamins and energy from their plant-based diet. It's not "gross for fun"; it's more like "gross for efficiency," which is still gross, but also kind of impressive.

Koalas have a famously picky diet of eucalyptus leaves, but baby koalas can't digest those tough leaves right away. To get the right gut microbes, a baby koala eats a special substance produced by its mother that helps seed its digestive system. The scientific explanation is fascinating. The car-ride explanation is: babies sometimes need... unusual snacks to grow up.

Vultures are basically nature's cleanup crew, and their habits show it. They eat carrion, which can contain dangerous bacteria. One reason they can do this is that their stomach acid is extremely strong, helping kill many pathogens. They also do something else that's startling but practical: vultures sometimes poop on their own legs. It can help cool them down and may reduce bacteria on their skin. If you're thinking, "There had to be another way," the vulture would probably respond, "I tried nothing and I'm all out of ideas."

Hippos look like gentle, chunky river cows, but their bathroom habits are pure chaos. When hippos poop, they often wag their tails rapidly, flinging the poop around to spread it. This can help mark territory and communicate. It's basically a messy, gross version of leaving a calling card, except the hippo's calling card is launched like a sprinkler.

Slugs and snails bring their own weirdness to romance. Many land snails are hermaphrodites, meaning they have both male and female reproductive organs. Some species even use something called a "love dart," a sharp structure one snail can jab into another during mating. It doesn't sound romantic, and it doesn't look romantic, but in snail world it's a whole strategy for increasing reproductive success. If humans did this, there would be a lot more "no thanks" in dating.

Beavers have a smell-based secret that people often misunderstand. They produce a substance called castoreum from glands near their tails, and they use it to mark territory. Castoreum has been used historically in perfumery and flavoring, and it has a vanilla-like scent. This fact always makes people squint and say, "Wait... what?" and that reaction is exactly why it belongs in a car-ride trivia book.

Dogs spin in circles before they lie down for reasons that may connect to their wild ancestors. Flattening grass, checking scents, and making a comfy spot could all play a part. Your dog might be doing a tiny ancient ritual on your living room rug, except it looks like it's trying to summon a nap.

Even honey has a slightly gross origin story, depending on how you feel about the word "regurgitate." Bees collect nectar and store it in a special stomach called a crop. Back at the hive, they pass it to other bees, who process it and evaporate water until it becomes honey. It's teamwork. It's chemistry. It's also, technically, bees sharing a snack mouth-to-mouth until it turns into something delicious.

The animal kingdom doesn't do "too gross." It does "whatever works." Once you start seeing it that way, you can laugh, say "eww," and still be amazed at how brilliantly weird life can be.

Escape Artists and Sneaky Superpowers

If you think animals live calm, cozy lives, imagine being a snack for something bigger every day. Many creatures survive by becoming experts in disappearing, tricking, or grossing out their enemies. Some of their moves sound like cartoon logic, except they're real—and they work.

A classic example is the lizard that can drop its tail to escape. In many lizard species, the tail can detach when grabbed, wriggling around to distract a predator while the lizard runs away. Later, the tail can regrow, though it may not look exactly the same. It's like leaving behind a decoy toy so you can sprint to safety, except your decoy is part of your own body. Nature is dramatic.

Opossums made "playing dead" famous, and it's not just acting. When threatened, some opossums can go into a state called thanatosis, where they appear dead and unresponsive. They may also release a foul-smelling fluid that makes them even less appealing. Predators that prefer fresh prey may lose interest. It's the animal version of saying, "You can't fire me, I already quit," while lying perfectly still.

Hagfish take the award for the grossest escape plan that is also oddly brilliant. When threatened, hagfish can produce large amounts of slime. The slime can clog a predator's gills and make it hard to breathe, forcing the attacker to back off. This isn't a tiny blob of slime, either; it can expand dramatically in water. It's like deploying an instant "nope cloud."

Cuttlefish and octopuses can release ink as a distraction. The ink can create a dark cloud that blocks vision, and sometimes it can form a decoy shape. While the predator is confused, the animal jets away. This is one reason these creatures seem like underwater magicians. They don't just vanish; they throw a smoke bomb first.

Some insects go for a strategy called "startle display," which is basically jump-scaring a predator. Certain moths and butterflies have wing patterns that look like big eyes. When they suddenly flash those wings open, a bird may hesitate just long enough for the insect to escape. It's the same principle as someone yelling "BOO!" and sprinting away, except the costume is built into your wings.

Archerfish have a skill that feels like it was designed for a carnival game. They can shoot a jet of water from their mouths to knock insects off branches above the water. Then they eat the insect after it falls. Hitting a target with a water "spit shot" takes good aim, and archerfish can adjust for distance. If fish held competitions, archerfish would be the ones winning prizes and bragging about it.

The Texas horned lizard has one of the most bizarre defenses ever documented: it can shoot blood from its eyes. When threatened, it can increase blood pressure in vessels near the eyes and squirt blood outward. The blood may taste bad to some predators. If you thought your sibling had a dramatic reaction to being teased, meet the lizard who literally weaponized drama.

Pufferfish don't run away; they inflate. By gulping water (or air, if out of water), they can puff up to look larger and harder to swallow. Many pufferfish also have spines, turning themselves into a prickly balloon. It's a simple idea with a strong message: "I am not bite-sized anymore."

And then there are animals that survive by being annoyingly hard to find. Stick insects blend in like twigs. Leaf-tailed geckos look like dead leaves. Some frogs resemble moss. Camouflage can be so effective that predators stare right at the animal and still don't see it. If you've ever lost a snack in the car and it mysteriously "vanished," you understand the pain predators feel.

These survival tricks aren't just weird. They're proof that the world is full of living problem-solvers—some of them slimy, some of them sneaky, and some of them equipped with built-in escape hatches.

Tiny Creatures, Huge Drama

Big animals get the documentaries, but tiny creatures often bring the most outrageous plot twists. Small bodies have to deal with big dangers, so many little animals evolved extreme abilities that feel like overkill in the best way.

Tardigrades, also known as water bears, are microscopic animals with a reputation for being almost indestructible. They can survive extreme conditions by entering a state called cryptobiosis, basically powering down until conditions improve. Some tardigrades have survived exposure to space-like conditions, intense cold, and dehydration. They're tiny, squishy-looking, and somehow tougher than most action heroes.

The mantis shrimp is not actually a shrimp, but it does have a punch that makes people's jaws drop. Some mantis shrimp have club-like limbs that strike so fast they can smash hard-shelled prey. The strike is so rapid it can create a phenomenon called cavitation, forming bubbles that collapse with enough force to add extra impact. In plain car-ride terms, it's like a tiny underwater boxer whose punch comes with bonus explosion bubbles.

A flea can jump astonishing distances compared to its body size. Fleas use a spring-like structure in their legs and store energy to launch themselves. For their size, their jumps are enormous, which helps them move between hosts. If humans could jump like fleas, a trip to the mailbox would involve clearing rooftops.

Ants can be surprisingly strong for their size, and their teamwork is even wilder. Some ants form living bridges with their bodies so the colony can cross gaps. Others link together to make rafts during floods. There are ants that farm fungi, ants that herd aphids, and ants that wage wars with neighboring colonies. If you ever hear someone say, "It's just an ant," you can reply, "Actually, it might be a tiny engineer with a complicated social life."

Spiders get a lot of fear, but jumping spiders deserve a moment of admiration. They have excellent vision compared to many other spiders and can leap with impressive accuracy. Some even perform tiny courtship dances, waving their legs and showing off colorful markings. Yes, somewhere out there, a spider is doing a dance routine to impress a date, and it's working.

The pistol shrimp makes sound effects that seem impossible for something so small. It can snap a specialized claw shut so fast that it creates a bubble, and when that bubble collapses, it produces a loud "pop" and a shockwave. In some cases, the collapsing bubble can briefly create extremely high temperatures in a tiny spot. It's like a miniature noisemaker that comes with science.

Even caterpillars bring drama. Some caterpillars have hairs or spines that can irritate predators. Others look like bird poop as camouflage, which is both hilarious and effective. Many caterpillars spend their whole early life eating nonstop, basically preparing for the most famous makeover in nature. If that doesn't deserve a reality show, what does?

Hummingbirds are small, but they're flying machines. Their wings can beat incredibly fast, and they can hover like tiny helicopters. They have high metabolisms and need frequent fuel, which is why they love nectar. Watching one zip around flowers is like watching a living jewel with an engine.

And then there's the bombadier beetle, which sounds like it belongs in a comic book. It can spray a hot, noxious chemical mixture at predators from its abdomen as a defense. The beetle stores chemicals separately and mixes them when needed, creating a rapid reaction that shoots the spray outward. It's basically a tiny creature carrying its own built-in chemistry lab, ready for emergencies.

Tiny animals remind you of an important rule of Earth: size does not predict weirdness. Sometimes the smallest creatures have the most over-the-top strategies, the most surprising talents, and the biggest "wait, what?!" moments.

If you want to turn this chapter into a quick car game, try this: after each fact, pause and ask who in the car thinks the animal sounds most like a superhero, a villain, or a comedian. You might end up with a whole cast of characters before the next exit.

2

SPACE STUFF THAT'LL BLOW YOUR MIND

Wild Weather on Other Worlds

If you strapped a weather station to a rocket and rode across space, you'd see a sky that never stops surprising. Planets have weather that would make Earth blink, and the kinds of storms we're talking about would look like nature's biggest, loudest, most dramatic shows—only with more gravity and less air to slow things down. The solar system is a catalog of wild atmospheres where wind speeds layer into the hundreds of miles per hour and storms last longer than a season or three on Earth. It's a reminder that "weather" isn't just what you wear to stay dry; it's how a world breathes and shouts through its own atmosphere.

Take Jupiter, for instance. Its Great Red Spot isn't a one-day weather event. It's a storm that's brewed for centuries, a gigantic swirl that dwarfs our entire planet. The winds around the spot whip around at hundreds of miles per hour, turning the giant's upper atmosphere into a roiling canyon of liquid air and color. If you were riding along in a hypothetical storm-chasing capsule, you'd see bands of clouds stretching to the horizon, with eye-like calm in the center and a surrounding hurricane of jet streams that seems to go on forever. The scale is so enormous that Earth would fit inside that storm dozens of times, and yet it's only one feature of a living, breathing world—one storm among many ordinary weather events on gas giants that never see snow because their skies are always a color other than white.

Saturn brings its own show: a hexagonal jet stream around its north pole. The shape is so unusual that scientists still marvel at how a six-sided sculpture of winds can exist on a spinning planet. The storm is hundreds of times larger than our planet, its boundaries calm and orderly in places while the winds whip around in a furious, synchronized dance. The winds can push faster than a hurricane on Earth, and the calm center of the hexagon is a strange counterpoint to the chaos immediately outside. It's as if Saturn wears a geometric crown made of air and time, a reminder that winds don't just curl—they can organize space itself into patterns we can observe from millions of miles away.

Beyond Jupiter and Saturn lie the outer worlds that look almost unreal when you picture their weather. Uranus tilts almost on its side, so what counts as a "season" is more like a planetary year-long limbo where one pole gets the sun for decades while the other sits in darkness. The winds of Uranus are strong, but they're not alone in their weirdness; Neptune roams the windy end of the spectrum with some of the fastest atmospheric chases in the solar system, where storms can unleash gusts that would cripple anything built by humans. The combination of tremendous winds, extreme temperatures, and alien rotation rates makes weather on these ice giants feel less like a forecast and more like a cosmic mixtape that never ends.

If you're imagining a world with runaway skies and storms that could swallow a mountain, you're not far off. Venus offers a different kind of weather show: an atmosphere so dense and hot that the surface temperature could melt lead, and clouds that swirl in a perpetual rain of sulfuric acid. The atmosphere spins around the planet with a speed that outpaces the planet's own rotation, so a day on Venus stretches longer than a year, creating a climate where the sun climbs over the horizon and never really stays low. The clouds glow with a glow you can see from space, a constant reminder that a planet can be hot, scary, and still somehow beautiful.

Even Mars has weather, though it's a much thinner show than the gas giants. Dust storms sweep across the red landscape, lifting dust high into the sky and bending the light into a dusty red haze that can shroud the surface for days or weeks. On a long drive, you might imagine a Mars storm blurring the horizon, a giant tumbleweed in a world where the air is so thin you could shout and hardly hear your own voice.

And while we're on the subject of weather, let's peek at the idea of exoplanets—the planets that orbit other stars. In our imaginations, some worlds might have rain made of molten glass or winds that howl at hundreds of miles per hour because they bake in the heat of their suns. The weather on these distant worlds isn't something we measure with thermometers on Earth; it's deduced through light curves, spectra, and clever physics. The picture is wild and often speculative, but it opens a door: if our solar system can host this many dramatic weather patterns, what kinds of storms exist out there in the galaxy? The answer is part science, part science fiction, and it's exactly the kind of spark that turns a road trip into a planet-sized adventure.

All of this isn't just trivia. It's a reminder that Earth, with its gentle breezes and occasional thunderstorm, sits inside a solar system where every planet has its own weather personality. The next time you see a cloud streak across the sky, try imagining what a storm would look like on Jupiter, or how the hexagon at Saturn's pole could glow in a color you've never seen up close. The universe loves to surprise us, not with a single favorite weather report, but with a whole menu of cosmic forecasts—each one stranger and more spectacular than the last.

Stars, Supernovas, and Boom

Stars are not just twinkling points in the night. They are vast nuclear furnaces, steady for eons and capable of surprises that echo across the cosmos. A star begins inside a cold, dark cloud of gas and dust called a nebula. Gravity pulls atoms together, and as material clumps into a protostar, the temperature climbs. When the core temperatures become hot enough, hydrogen starts to fuse into helium, and the star lights up. From that moment, it becomes a factory of energy, shining for billions of years as it balances gravity's pull with the pressure from fusion inside.

Our Sun is a typical example of a middle-aged star, a gassy sphere bright enough to keep a solar system in order. Its surface glows at roughly 5,500 degrees Celsius, while its core roars at tens of millions of degrees. It's a swarm of activity: light, heat, solar wind—the continuous outflow of charged particles that shapes planets, comets, and the very edge of the solar system. Stars come in a dazzling range of sizes and colors. Blue stars are the hottest, followed by white, yellow, orange, and red stars. The color tells you what temperature the star's surface holds, which in turn hints at its mass and life story.

But stars don't stay the same forever. A star like the Sun will eventually run out of hydrogen to fuse. It will puff up into a red giant, shedding its outer layers before finally capping off its life as a white dwarf—the cooling ember of a once-bright engine. More massive stars live in a more dramatic world, ending their lives in brilliant cataclysms called supernovas. A core-collapse supernova happens when the core of a massive star collapses under its own gravity, triggering an explosion so powerful it can briefly outshine an entire galaxy. The blast is more than just spectacle; it sails the cosmos with elements like carbon and iron, which later become part of new stars, planets, and even life itself. In the aftermath, what's left can be a neutron star—an incredibly dense remnant spinning so fast that it acts like a cosmic lighthouse—or, if the mass is enough, a black hole bending the very fabric of space.

There are other kinds of cosmic fireworks too. A white dwarf in a binary system can siphon material from a neighbor, triggering a nova—a sudden brightening that lights up the night in a temporarily new way. In the most extreme cases, a star's death can unleash a gamma-ray burst, a flash so intense that it briefly outshines all other galaxies in the observable universe and sends jets of energy racing across space at nearly light speed. It's hard to overstate the scale of these events: a single supernova enriches the universe with the heavier elements that make up planets, oceans, and the people reading these words.

Distances in space are so vast that we measure them in light-years—the distance light travels in one year. That's why a star can show us how it looked many millions of years ago; the light we see now is the story of what the star was like long before we existed. The cosmos runs on time scales that dwarf human lifetimes, yet the effects of these stellar dances echo in every corner of the universe. The life cycle of stars is a reminder that endings are not quiet, simple things. They are transitions that scatter the seeds for new beginnings, and those seeds will someday grow into the next generation of suns, planets, and perhaps life again.

There are times when science feels like a fireworks show designed by someone with a sense of humor. A small star can live longer than a big one, but when the big ones end, they end with a bang that invites the whole galaxy to watch. Smaller explosions, like novas, are a reminder that even the little things in space have a dramatic side. Gamma-ray bursts, the most intense events in the universe since the Big Bang, stretch our imagination about what can be possible in a cosmos that is constantly rewriting its own rules. And then there are the quiet, ordinary moments—the steady glow of stars that have burned for billions of years and will burn for billions more—reminding us that there is both thunder and lullaby in the night sky.

Space Is Loud (In a Weird Way)

Space is famously silent. It is a vacuum, which means there isn't air to carry sound the way it does on Earth. If you shouted in the void between stars, your voice would disappear into the quiet, fading before it could even travel a few feet. That's a hard truth for kids who grew up with soundtracks and whooshy noises in their headphones. Yet space isn't truly quiet. It hums in its own language—the language of waves and fields and particles—and clever humans have learned to translate those signals into sounds we can hear.

Radio waves carry information across space much like waves carry sound on a windy shore. Scientists scoop up those radio waves with antennas and turn them into audio files you can listen to. When you hear the sound made from a solar storm or a pulsar's steady ticking, you're listening to a human-made interpretation of the universe's own music. A pulsar, for instance, is a star that spins incredibly fast and beams radiation like a cosmic lighthouse. Its pulses arrive with clockwork regularity, a rhythm you can hear if you translate the signal into sound. It's not actual sound in space, but it's a useful, mind-bending way to understand how quickly the cosmos can move.

The solar wind—streams of charged particles blowing outward from the Sun—also makes sounds of a kind when translated. It interacts with the magnetic fields around planets, creating auroras that light up the poles in ribbons of color on Earth and other worlds. If you could hear the space around us, you'd hear a quiet, bouncy chorus of radio whistles, crackles, and pops representing different sources—an electro-acoustic portrait of a universe that is, in many ways, loud and alive, just not with sound the way we traditionally hear it.

In classrooms, listeners, and car rides, this concept becomes a playful puzzle. Space is silent but loud through the information it carries, and scientists are the translators who turn that information into the music of the spheres. The idea helps us realize that listening isn't only about ears; it's about asking questions, following signals, and turning them into stories you can share on a road trip. Space becomes not a vacuum to fear but a grand orchestra to explore, a reminder that the universe has a voice—and that voice is full of wonder.

The Moon Isn't Boring

The Moon isn't a dull, grey rock waiting to be ignored on a clear night. It's a complex world with a history that's written in craters and lava plains, a natural satellite that has shaped the way we live on Earth. Our Moon is slowly drifting away from us, at a pace of about 3.8 centimeters per year. That may not sound like much, but given enough time, it adds up to intriguing consequences for tides, orbital dynamics, and the future of Earth's climate. If you picture a long road trip, it's like the Moon gradually stepping back from the window, changing the view you've grown used to over generations.

The Moon is a world of contrasts. On the near side, you'll find vast seas of basalt called maria that were created by ancient lava flows. They give the Moon its familiar, pockmarked map of dark patches set against bright highlands. The far side is more cratered and rugged, a reminder that not all sides of worlds are the same even when gravity keeps them bound together. This difference makes the Moon brilliantly photogenic and endlessly interesting to scientists who study how planets and moons evolve under different conditions.

One reason the Moon feels so alive in a family car conversation is the way it moves. It's tidally locked to Earth, which means we always see the same face—a face that changes only through slow libration, a tiny wobble that reveals a bit more of the far side from time to time. The Moon's gravity also tugs on Earth, shaping our tides and helping stabilize our planet's tilt, which in turn helps keep our seasons from spinning out of control.

The Moon is also a laboratory and a playground. It has quakes—moonquakes—some due to cooling, some triggered by tidal forces, and some by meteorite impacts. It also hides water in cold pockets near its poles, a surprising clue about how water could exist in surprising places. The rocks brought back by Apollo astronauts whisper stories of a time when Earth and the Moon shared a much more chaotic youth, and those samples still teach scientists about the early solar system. The Moon remains a source of awe and a destination that invites families to imagine future adventures—base camps on the Moon, science tests under a pale Earthshine, and the simple joy of watching a neighbor world drift through the night.

3

THE HUMAN BODY'S FUNNIEST GLITCHES

Strange Senses

Our senses aren't just a handful of easy presets. They're a bustling orchestra that sometimes plays tricks on you just as you're cruising down the highway. Your nose, your tongue, your skin, your eyes, and your ears are constantly trading signals with your brain, and sometimes the signal gets a little squiggly. It's not a glitch so much as life's playful design—your body leaning into curiosity with a wink.

Smell is a surprising star of show-and-tell. The nose can detect a huge range of scents, and it isn't shy about how memories hitch a ride with aroma. Some scientists toss around the idea of up to a trillion possible odors, while others land closer to thousands or millions. Either way, a whiff of something familiar can unlock a flood of memories and feelings in an instant. It's that strong connection between scent and memory that makes grandma's kitchen smell like a winter morning even years later.

Taste is the other side of flavor, a chemistry set that lives on your tongue and in your head. Our taste buds come in a few flavors—sweet, sour, salty, bitter, and the savory richness humans call umami. You have about ten thousand taste buds at your peak, and they're constantly replacing themselves every week or two. The idea that the tongue alone decides what you taste isn't quite right, though. The brain is doing a lot of the heavy lifting, fusing signals from your tongue with your nose, texture, temperature, and even your mood. That's why something as simple as soup can feel totally different on a sleepy afternoon versus a busy morning.

Touch is the body's most intimate language. The skin is the largest organ, and it's dotted with nerve endings that tell your brain about pressure, temperature, pain, and even subtle textures. Your fingertips are particularly chatty, which is why you can guess whether something is velvet or coarse sand with a single swipe. Proprioception —the sense that tells you where your body is in space— works like an internal GPS. Close your eyes, touch your fingertip to your nose, and you'll feel it as clearly as you see it. The car hits a bump and your balance system whispers a reminder to stay upright; even a gentle turn requires the brain to coordinate eyes, ears, and muscles in perfect harmony.

Your inner ear runs a tiny, magical committee on balance. The vestibular system senses motion, direction, and gravity, and it's the reason you feel a bit wobbly after a roller coaster or a long car ride that twists and stops in a snap. Spin in a chair and your world tilts; it's your brain trying to keep everything steady while your eyes chase the scenery outside the window. This is also why you sometimes pause a moment before you answer a question when the car lurches or the sun blinds you for a second.

Goosebumps aren't just dramatic hair. They're the body's little go-to trick for staying warm or looking bigger to a possible threat. Tiny muscles jump into action along each hair follicle, making each hair stand up like a tiny antenna. It's not glamorous, but it's a stubbornly efficient reflex developed by generations who wore thicker coats and heavier fur. In modern days, goosebumps can still appear in chilly air, during scary moments in a movie, or when you hear a sappy song that somehow hits the nostalgia button just right.

A few quirks of our senses come dressed as tiny glitches. You can't tickle yourself the way someone else can because your brain predicts your own touch with uncanny accuracy. The brain programs the sensation and cancels the surprise, which is why a back pat from a friend always feels a lot funnier than your own hand brushing your belly. The sense of smell can fade in a chorus of familiar odors after a few minutes, leaving a scentless quiet that makes new smells feel like a "wow" again. And taste can shift with mood and context; the same bite can feel different depending on whether you're hungry, tired, or stuck in a long line at the grocery store.

These strange senses aren't trying to trick you so much as inviting you to notice the world more carefully. Imagine you're in the passenger seat, window cracked, and a breeze brushing your face. You can point out a hundred tiny signals—the temperature drop on a chilly day, a sour note in a fruit you've never recognized before, the moment you realize the car's air freshener is doing a little dance with your nose. It's not just trivia; it's a way to tune your attention to what's around you and make ordinary moments feel a touch more magical.

So when you're on a road trip pretending not to be bored, look closer at what your senses are doing. Notice the way your eyes adapt to light as you pass a row of trees. Listen for the faint hum of the engine and the soft whisper of tires on asphalt. Smell the piney scent of a fresh air vent or the whiff of rain that sometimes tastes like clean electricity on the tongue. Your body's glitches are not failures; they're invitations to observe, guess, laugh, and share what you notice with the people in the car.

Now, take a moment and test a tiny brain trick you can do right in the backseat. Close your eyes for a few seconds and breathe in slowly through your nose. Can you name the five basic tastes you just experienced in your mouth? If not, that's a perfect moment to giggle and assign a playful guess. The point isn't perfection; it's curiosity, conversation, and the kind of attention that turns a drive into a mini-adventure for everyone listening.

Bones, Bumps, and Bendy Bits

The human skeleton is a living framework that's strong, flexible, and a little bit silly in the way it handles everyday life. It holds you upright, protects your organs, and somehow keeps your body's secret trick book ready for action—like a team of tiny, tireless construction workers who never take a break. And yes, it also has a few goofy quirks that make you say, "Wait, what?" while you're waiting at a stoplight.

Starting with the bones themselves, you're born with roughly 270 bones. As you grow, some of these bones fuse together, and by adulthood you'll usually settle on around 206 bones. That's a lot of parts, all cooperating to let you stand, run, dance, and webinar-facetiously dodge a flying football. The skeleton isn't a solid statue either; it's a living system that constantly remodels itself—the old bone is removed and replaced by new bone in a careful, ongoing cycle. This is how bones stay strong and respond to life's demands, whether you're sprinting for the bus or carrying groceries with a wobbly tote.

A surprising bit of the skeleton's drama happens when you wake up. In the morning, you're a touch taller than you'll be by night. The reason is simple: the discs in your spine soak up water as you rest, expanding a little like little sponges. When you're vertical and busy all day, gravity squeezes them down again, and you end up a tiny bit shorter by evening. It's not dramatic, but it's a neat reminder that your body is a dynamic machine, not a single, fixed statue.

There are 206 bones in an average adult, and each one has a story. Some bones are long and strong like the femur in your thigh, which can bear a lot of weight and strain. Others are tiny and light, like the bones that make up your inner ear—malleus, incus, and stapes—that help you hear the world in delicate detail. Some bones are paired as left and right halves, while others, like the hyoid bone in your throat, aren't directly connected to any other bone. The hyoid floats in place, anchored by muscles and ligaments, and it helps with speaking and swallowing in a way that feels almost magical until you realize it's just physics in disguise.

The joints that connect bones are where the body really gets flexible. Cartilage cushions the ends of bones, making it possible to bend your knees, wrists, and elbows without grinding every time you move. Sometimes you hear popping sounds—that cracking you hear when you straighten a finger or crack a knuckle is gas bubbles forming and bursting in the joints, something scientists call crepitus. It's perfectly harmless most of the time, though a bit loud for a quiet car ride if you're the one doing the cracking.

You can't ignore the teeth when you're counting bones, either. Your adult set typically consists of 32 teeth, designed to bite, chew, and help shape your smile. Those teeth aren't just for looks; they're also a reminder that your body has to manage both hard bone and resilient enamel. Teeth come in from an early age and make a journey that ends with wisdom teeth sometimes arriving late—and sometimes never needed if they decide to stay out of the party.

A body fact that borders on the funny is how our bodies wear their hair and nails. Hair and nails are made of keratin, the same tough protein that gives us our nails a little extra shine in the sun. They grow whether we're running in summer heat or stuck in a winter's line at the grocery store. Nails and hair don't bounce back when you cut them; they simply keep growing from living cells at their roots, which is a tiny reminder that even "dead" tissues still have a job in a living person.

In the end, your bones and bending bits are one big, coordinated circus act. They hold you up, keep you moving, and perhaps occasionally surprise you with a crack, a pop, or a surprising capacity to stretch a little more than you thought. When you're driving, admire the little wonders as you squat, stretch, or step out at a rest stop. Your bones are the backstage crew—quiet, steady, and always ready for the next act.

For a quick curiosity starter, imagine you're the director of your own body. If you could redesign your skeleton for a day, what would you want more of—height to reach the top shelf, extra joint flexibility to bend around car seats, or tougher bones to survive a fall? The questions are playful, but the answers reveal how cool and capable our bodies really are, even when they do a few silly things.

From the tiniest ear bone to the longest leg bone, our skeleton's blend of strength, flexibility, and a few goofy quirks makes daily life a little more interesting. The more you know about how your body works, the more you'll spot the funny, surprising things going on every moment of every ride.

Belly and Bathroom Trivia

If you listen closely on a long drive, your belly might start its own conversation. The digestive system is basically a smart, efficient factory, turning random food into energy, while also giving you enough giggles to keep the car interesting. Digestion is one of those everyday processes you barely notice until something goes wrong, and then suddenly you're acutely aware of every rumble, gurgle, and burp that follows.

The stomach has a powerful job, and it keeps its defenses sharp with a protective mucous layer. The lining is coated to withstand harsh acid and enzymes as it churns and mixes your meal into a semi-liquid soup called chyme. This lining is continually renewed, so the stomach doesn't eat itself in the process. It's a smart, self-care system that works quietly in the background while you're telling a joke or shouting out a stream of song lyrics at a rest stop. This is why the truck-stop meal doesn't always revolt; the body is authoring a backstage pass that keeps things calm under pressure.

From there, chyme slides into the small intestine, a long, winding tube that stretches about twenty feet in an adult. Here, nutrients get swallowed up by the wall's tiny finger-like projections called villi, which act like a sponge for energy and building blocks the rest of your body can use. The small intestine is where most of the magic happens, dissolving fats, carbohydrates, and proteins into ready-to-use fuel. It's also a cheerful reminder that your body is more than just a stomach; it's a living workshop with many rooms working in synchrony.

The liver deserves a gold star for multitasking. It metabolizes nutrients, filters toxins, stores energy, and even makes bile, the greenish stuff that helps digest fats. The gallbladder is the little pouch that stores some of that bile until it's needed, like a tiny kitchen for a busy chef who plates meals in moments. Meanwhile, the pancreas releases enzymes into the small intestine, turning big molecules into the smaller pieces your body can actually use. It's a busy team trying to keep you running, even on a road trip with popcorn as a constant companion.

The large intestine finishes the job, pulling water from leftovers and turning what's left into stool. The gut isn't just a waste station; it's also a haven for trillions of bacteria that help with digestion and even talk to your immune system. These microbes aren't villains; they're tiny partners that keep you running smoothly. And yes, sometimes your belly has opinions about what you've eaten. A growl here, a rumble there, and you're reminded that your insides aren't shy about making themselves heard.

A quick mental game you can play while the engine hums is guessing what each sound means. If your stomach growls loudly after a break for chips, is it simply saying hello to the air you just swallowed, or is it editorializing about a thought you had five minutes ago? Either way, your body is narrating the ride with a chorus of sounds that feel like a tiny in-car soundtrack. And when you need to explain your timing to a curious passenger, you can say it's just the kitchen inside your stomach rehearsing for the next big scene.

The digestive system is built for speed and resilience. Food moves from mouth to exhale with a rhythm that can feel almost musical. If you're watching the scenery, you might forget about the work being done behind the scenes. But as soon as you take a bite and the teeth start chewing in earnest, the whole car becomes part of a grand, messy, marvelous biological concert. The more you notice, the more you realize how the body can do complex things with surprising ease, even when you're stuck in a car with a backseat full of questions and a chorus of "are we there yet?"

Finally, a reminder that digestion isn't just about fuel. It's a story about how your body keeps moving, growing, and repairing itself every single day. The gut tells a tale of balance, efficiency, and adaptation—the kind of story that makes ordinary meals feel like an adventure in disguise. So next time you're munching a snack or sipping a drink, pause to listen to the tiny world inside your belly and appreciate the science and humor behind every burp, burble, and buzz that follows.

Brain Quirks

The brain is the most remarkable organ in the car for a reason. It's constantly solving puzzles, managing a million little tasks, and sometimes dropping a clue that makes you grin or gasp. It's also prone to little glitches that keep life funny and interesting. Understanding these quirks can make riding in the car feel less like a routine and more like a front row seat to a comedy of mind and memory.

One classic brain trick is change blindness. If you're focused on a task, you might miss big visual changes right in front of you. This isn't stubbornness of the eyes; it's the brain's way of conserving attention for what seems most important at that moment. You may stare right at a friend's new hat and not even notice when the car seat suddenly changes color or a large poster on the wall swaps to a different image. It's a reminder that our perception is a selection process, not a video camera recording every single detail.

Then there's inattentional blindness, a cousin of change blindness. When you're concentrating on one thing—like counting the number of red cars on the road—the brain may miss something obvious in your peripheral vision. Picture this: a waiter walks by with a tray, or a gorilla strolls across a screen, and you don't notice it because your brain is busy with something else. It's funny in hindsight, and it's a great prompt for a "spot the odd thing" game in the car.

The tip-of-the-tongue phenomenon is another crowd-pleaser. You're sure you know the word, you can picture the exact sound, but it won't come out. It's moments like these that spark giggles and quick guessing games, and they remind us that memory is a fragile, fallible friend. We remember the gist—the story, the vibe, the punchline—not every precise letter, and that's perfectly normal.

Memory itself is a sculptor, not a camera. Recollection is reconstructive; each time you remember something, your brain rebuilds it using the best parts available, sometimes stitching in new details along the way. The Mandela Effect—where many people remember something in a way that turns out to be wrong—can become a hilarious, shared stretch of road-trip lore. It's not about being right; it's about turning memory into something you can talk about for miles and miles.

Your brain also loves patterns and shortcuts. The Stroop effect asks you to name the color of the word rather than read the word itself, which creates a tiny, playful mental traffic jam. It's a small reminder that the mind doesn't always follow the freshest logic under pressure. In the car, these moments are perfect excuses to pause and laugh: a friend misreads a familiar label, a mini-puzzle of letters and colors that becomes a shared joke at the next rest stop.

But not all quirks are tricks of memory. The brain's built-in social antenna, the cocktail party effect, helps you tune into a friend's voice in a noisy room. In a family car, that means you can pick out the one person speaking in a chorus of siblings, even if you'd rather listen to the radio. It's not magic; it's neural engineering in action, a small miracle you get to witness in real time as you swap stories and jokes with the people you love.

Phantom sensations also have a place in the backseat. Have you ever felt your phone vibrate in your pocket when it's not actually buzzing? The brain's patterns can create sensations that feel real even when they're not. It's a reminder that the mind sometimes engineers its own little show, a harmless phantasm that makes you look twice at a simple notification you thought you'd ignored.

All these quirks are not misfires; they're features that give our brains character and humor. They explain why a road trip can become a narrative of tiny moments—spotting a bird, misreading a road sign, or remembering someone's joke in the exact moment you need a laugh. The brain's creativity is a constant source of surprises, and in the car, those surprises are built into every mile.

To wrap up this chapter, remember this: curiosity is a superpower when you're on a ride. Use the brain's quirks to spark conversations, games, and small experiments with memory. Challenge each other to spot a change, guess a word you know you know, or recount a childhood memory that morphs with each telling. The goal isn't perfect recall; it's shared wonder, a few good laughs, and a few more questions to chase on the next stretch of road.

4

HISTORY'S STRANGEST MOMENTS (YES, REALLY)

Royal Ridiculousness

History isn't just dates and marching armies; sometimes it's a long parade of odd rules, quirky habits, and scandals that feel like they were written for a comedy sketch. When you're driving past a farm, an castle, a museum, or even a palace in your imagination, you're passing by the same moments that made rulers act in surprising ways, show off power in ridiculous ways, or just stumble into the kind of "you couldn't make this up" stories that kids and adults love to repeat. These tales aren't mean; they're curious. They show that the people at the top of the food chain—kings, queens, emperors, and pop-eyed court ministers—were humans with weird tastes, stubborn habits, and the kind of dramatic flair that makes history feel personal and, yes, funny.

Let's start with the idea that rulers sometimes wrote the rules at home so strange they felt like a game of dress-up gone wrong. Sumptuary laws are a perfect example. These were legal rules that told people what they could wear, how bright their fabrics could be, and even what colors signaled "rank." For centuries in medieval and early modern Europe, fashion policing became a way for the powerful to keep everyone in their lane. If you wore velvet when you were supposed to wear wool, you faced fines or social scorn. If you showed up with gold lace when your class wasn't supposed to have it, you could be in real trouble. It sounds almost comical today, but it was serious business. The courts weren't just ruling on policy; they were policing identity. Fashion became a political statement, and the front row of a royal audience turned into a runway where missteps could cost you status, wealth, or prestige. The idea was to remind people that the king's taste was sovereign. The reality, as you can imagine, looked more like a steady stream of petty tyranny and lavish expense, punctuated by the occasional social rebellion from a noble who wanted to push the limits just a little further.

Then there's a much less fictional moment in the drama of rulers: Peter the Great of Russia in the late 17th and early 18th centuries. He loved Western ideas, ships, and, famously, a good old beard. To modernize, he introduced a beard tax—yes, a tax on facial hair. The joke in the backseat of history is that you could either shave or pay up. For many nobles and merchants, this was a lighthearted but financially binding decision, a statement of allegiance to reform and a statement of wealth. The beard tax turned beards into receipts, and receipts into stories told at gatherings years later. It's a silly-sounding policy with surprisingly real consequences: if you wanted to keep your beard, you carried a token, you paid your tax, and you continued in your daily life with a new, somewhat humorous badge of identity. It's a reminder that big changes in history sometimes show up not as grand speeches but as small, stubborn acts like choosing whiskers over compliance.

And then we get the wild rumor mill of imperial theater. Caligula, the Roman emperor known for excess, allegedly did something so far-fetched it sounds almost cartoonish: he supposedly made his horse a consul. A consul was one of the highest political offices in Rome, the kind of role that helps steer a republic or an empire. Elevating a horse to that rank isn't something you call "policy" so much as "legend." It's a story that comes wrapped in "maybe true, maybe not," but its appeal is in the image: a ruler whose unlimited appetite for spectacle turns government into performance art. Whether true or not, the tale captures a truth about power: when you have unlimited sway, your whims can seem like decrees, and your house can feel less like a government building and more like a stage.

Even in the more dignified corners of kings and queens, there were moments of self-parody and instructions that feel almost scripted by a prankster. The great theatre of Versailles wasn't just about grand halls; it was a maze of etiquette and ritual. A single misstep could turn a noble into a cautionary tale. The levée, those daily morning rituals of waking, dressing, and presenting oneself to the king, turned into a social sport—the choreography of who bowed to whom, who spoke first, and how your shoes were polished to catch the light just right. The goal wasn't merely to show wealth or power; it was to demonstrate control of time itself. When every glance, gesture, and servant's movement seemed governed by a rulebook, the history of one court becomes the history of a living, breathing performance.

Finally, legends circle around the fabled "vomitorium" and other popular myths about ancient life. The idea that ancient Romans spent feasts vomiting to make room for more courses is a story that sticks in the imagination, even though it's not supported by reliable sources. The lesson is less about debunking and more about understanding how stories grow when people try to explain flamboyant life with sharp, memorable phrases. It's also a reminder that the people who lived long ago weren't merely "old-timey" versions of us; they were people with strange rules, odd priorities, and moments of ridiculousness that make their world feel surprisingly close to ours. History's ridiculousness isn't random; it's a window into how power, tradition, and personality rub up against life's simple human need to entertain, to outwit, and to surprise.

As you read, keep your eyes open for the thread that links all these moments: authority trying to stay polished on the surface while the people beneath it crave a little whimsy, a little rebellion, and a lot of conversation. In cars, on long drives, in a moment of family car karaoke or a quick stop at a scenic overlook, these stories become more than trivia. They become jumping-off points for questions, debates, and giggles—exactly the kind of fuel a backseat crew loves when the road stretches on and on.

Wars with Weird Causes

History isn't only about generals and battles; it's also about goofy, petty, or utterly surprising reasons that people went to war. Some conflicts began with something as small as a stray animal, a missing bucket, or a quarrel that spiraled into a full-blown clash. The point isn't to celebrate war but to marvel at how fragile human disagreements can become when pride, fear, and a dash of stubbornness take the wheel. These stories are the perfect kind of "are we there yet?" history—fast, fascinating, and easy to recall when you're stuck in traffic or sitting at a long red light.

The War of the Stray Dog is a famous example from the 1920s, a border incident between Greece and Bulgaria that started when a Greek soldier's dog wandered across the border. It sounds almost cute, but it escalated quickly. A simple canine misstep became a symbol of deeper tensions between two neighbors who had many grievances simmering beneath the surface. The dog didn't know it, but it had an outsized impact on diplomacy, turning a fragile moment into a demonstration of how quickly words on a map can become shouts on the ground. In a backseat game of hypothetical diplomacy, imagine your own family crossing a line with a pet — the same boundaries that govern a playful rabbit in the yard now drawn as a national border. The lesson here is that sometimes, the spark is something small, but the flame it lights can be big enough to warm or burn an entire region.

Another famous, almost comical-in-retrospect war is the Pig War of 1859. It began with a pig, a boisterous sow named "Sus," who belonged to a farmer on San Juan Island. The animal's death by gunshot did not have the solemn import of a treaty, but it set off a chain reaction. Each side sent ships, laid claims to the soil, and prepared for a confrontation that, in real terms, never quite became a full-blown battle. It's easy to chuckle at the image of soldiers arguing over a pig, yet the Pig War shows how quickly a clever smirk can become a stalemate. The resolution came not through a conclusive clash but through negotiation and patience, a reminder that some of history's quirkiest moments prove more about diplomacy and humor than about victory or defeat.

The War of Jenkins' Ear is another vivid example. It began with something as small as a severed ear on a sea captain's helmet. A Spanish ship cut off a British captain's ear in the Caribbean, and the two nations who had otherwise been friendly found themselves in a conflict named after an injury. The title itself feels almost like a cartoon, but the events that followed involved real battles, long sea voyages, and political maneuvering. It's a reminder that history often rides on the edge of personal insult, miscommunication, or a misread signal across a crowded room—or across a sea. We see how fragile lines can be, how easily a dispute can become a war when a calculator and a sword are both in the room, and how important it is still to choose conversation over escalation when possible.

The Emu War of 1932 is the modern punchline to this chapter of strange causes. Australia declared war on a flightless bird, a decision born of farmers' complaints about crop destruction. The operation wasn't a triumph of strategy; it was a misfit of logistics and nature. The emus proved to be remarkably resilient, and the humans, with their rifles and road networks, found themselves outpaced by the very birds they were trying to govern. It's a story that looks like a prank, and in many ways, it is—a reminder that nature is an opponent with a surprising sense of timing. The Emu War didn't re-shape borders or topple governments; it taught a few officials to keep a sense of humor, to recalibrate how to protect livelihoods, and to recognize that sometimes the best response is cooperation rather than confrontation.

We can't skip the "Football War" between El Salvador and Honduras, a short conflict that erupted after tense World Cup qualifying matches. The tension had built up for months, fueled by historical rivalries, immigration disputes, and media sensationalism. When the soccer pitch became the stage for real-world bravado, the sports world looked on in disbelief. The escalation shows how quickly a cultural moment—an intense football rivalry—can spill into political action. It's a reminder that sport can be a peaceful form of competition and a fierce spark for conflict in equal measure.

And then there's the War of the Oaken Bucket, a medieval skirmish sparked by something as humble as a bucket. The tale goes that a bucket was stolen during a river crossing, and the two Italian city-states of Modena and Bologna blamed each other for the slight. Soon the border was aflame with petty feuds, and the conflict dragged on for years over pride, pride, and the idea that who owned a bucket could determine the fate of a people. The lesson? Sometimes the best ending to a war is not a victory on a battlefield but a shared laugh, a difficult compromise, or simply letting someone else take the bucket, metaphorical or not.

All these moments remind us that history is filled with human beings trying to prove a point, defend a border, or simply win a bragging-rights contest. They show how fragile the line between rivalry and ridiculousness can be. In the car, they can become quick prompts for "What would you do if…?" challenges: imagine you're dean of a tiny kingdom with a rule about hats, or you're leading a squad into a pseudo-battle against a stubborn animal. The important part isn't the victory or the defeat; it's the conversation, the laughter, and the way a tiny incident becomes a big story we tell again and again.

Mistakes That Changed Everything

Some of history's biggest leaps forward came from mistakes so big they changed the world. They're the kind of stories that make you want to slam the brakes and talk through every turn, every choice, and every what-if. These are the moments when a wrong move becomes a right answer in disguise. They're not about blunders as punishment; they're about surprises that pushed humanity toward new ideas, new tools, and new ways of thinking. And the best part for a road trip: they're short, dramatic, and easy to remember, often starting with something as simple as curiosity and ending with something we now take for granted.

The first star we're going to hitch a ride with is Alexander Fleming and the accidental discovery of penicillin. In a lab crowded with bacteria, a simple lapse—leaving a petri dish uncovered—turned into a moment that would save millions of lives. A mold named Penicillium notatum settled on a dish containing Staphylococcus bacteria, and to Fleming's astonishment, the mold inhibited the growth around it. That slender green halo sparked a revolution in medicine. What began as a mundane, nearly forgettable day in the lab transformed into the era of antibiotics. It's a reminder that the path from curiosity to invention isn't always straight; it's a zigzag that often starts with an inadvertent spill, a moment of doubt, and a leap of faith.

Another world-changing blunder came when Goodyear decided to try a new mixture of rubber. Charles Goodyear was chasing a way to make rubber durable while remaining flexible, and his experiment went wrong in spectacular fashion. He spilled rubber on a hot stove, and instead of a ruined mess, he created vulcanized rubber. The process used sulfur to cross-link the molecules, giving rubber that could survive hot days, cold days, and all the rain and wear in between. It sounds like a mistake that happened to ruin a day, but it turned into the backbone of tires, seals, and countless everyday items we rely on. In a car ride, you can imagine the spark of that "oops" turning into a global network of wheels that keeps families moving on road trips.

Sometimes it's a snack that reshapes history. The potato chip was born when a chef named George Crum got fed up with a customer who kept sending back his fried potatoes, insisting they were too thick and soft. Crum's stubborn perfectionism led him to fry the potatoes until they were paper-thin, crisp, and irresistible. The result? A snack that would become a universal road-trip staple and a reminder that even a small quarrel can spark a breakthrough idea. The moral here is gentle: a stubborn moment can yield something delicious and lasting when you're open to a playful solution rather than a loud argument.

And then there's the story of the first X-ray image. Wilhelm Röntgen was experimenting with cathode rays and discovered something revolutionarily practical: a way to see inside the body without cutting it open. He wasn't hunting for a medical breakthrough; he was chasing better vacuum tubes. The accidental discovery of X-rays opened a window into the human body, changing medicine, surgery, and diagnostics forever. It's a reminder that a curious, careful, and sometimes accidental moment in a lab can illuminate the entire future of science and health. In a car, we can relate this to how the simplest questions—what happens if we look inside?—can lead to surprising answers that help everyone go safer and healthier.

Another classic turn occurs in the history of everyday technology: the microwaves that heat our food. Percy Spencer, an engineer working on radar, noticed that a candy bar in his pocket had melted while he stood near a magnetron. That tiny observation became the story of the microwave oven. What started as a single, personal moment grew into a household appliance that reshaped cooking, snacking, and the way families spend time together on road trips. It's a reminder that everyday devices often arrive at our feet through unusual experiments and unexpected results—sometimes when you're trying to do one thing, you end up inventing something entirely different.

The science of life offers another pair of examples. Fleming's penicillin is perhaps the most famous, but we can also look at the discovery of insulin by Frederick Banting and Charles Best in 1921. The process involved a lot of careful work, a bit of luck, and a willingness to follow a hunch. Insulin transformed diabetes from a devastating diagnosis into a treatable condition. It's the kind of moment that seems almost magical in retrospect, yet it began with a few scientists chasing clues in a laboratory and a stubborn dedication to unraveling a mystery. In the car, this serves as a reminder that questions—hunted or stumbled upon—can lead to life-changing breakthroughs when we keep exploring rather than giving up.

The thread tying all these stories together is clear: mistakes aren't the end; they're the doorway to progress when they're treated as opportunities to learn. They invite us to look at what seemed accidental and to ask, "What if we looked closer? What if we tried one more time?" That mindset is perfect for road trips, where the best moments often involve a quick rethink, a new plan, or a playful detour that reveals something marvelous about the world around us.

So when the kids complain that the road is boring, you can tell them about the magic hidden in missteps—a moldy dish and a laughing scientist, a farmer's stubborn chip, and a spark that lit up entire centuries. You can show that history is less about perfection and more about curiosity, resilience, and the courage to try again, no matter how many wrong turns you think you've taken.

Everyday Life Back Then

The past isn't a distant land of candlelight and cranky streetlamps; it's a world where some of the little things in daily life look hilariously different from today—and sometimes a little bit gross, too. When you're in the backseat, imagine stepping out of your car and stepping into a time machine where the smells, sounds, and routines aren't what you're used to. The aim isn't to frighten or overwhelm, but to show kids how smart, adaptable, and curious people have always had to be, even when their houses didn't run on Wi-Fi and their days started well before the sun stopped rising.

Let's start with home and family life. Indoor plumbing was a later invention, and many households relied on outhouses, chamber pots, and separate rooms for chores you'd expect to see in a museum. Bathing wasn't a daily habit for most families; people often bathed only a few times a week, sometimes even less, depending on the era and the city. Showerheads didn't exist in the way we know them, and running hot water could be as scarce as a quiet moment in a crowded car ride. The practical upshot is simple: families planned their days around when water could be heated, heated, and hauled from a well or a nearby stream. If you're stuck in a long drive with kids who want baths and snacks at every exit, you can remind them that our modern comforts weren't always guaranteed, and that makes the everyday chores we do now feel like a luxury we should celebrate.

School and learning looked different, too. In many places, children learned on slate boards with chalk, or they copied passages from big, heavy books rather than tapping at tablets. Homework might involve memorizing multiplication tables by rote or reciting passages aloud to the entire family, who would listen with a mix of pride and exasperation. There weren't endless online videos to help with a tricky problem; help came from teachers, siblings, or a neighbor who loved the same subject you did. It's a reminder that knowledge is a social act as much as a personal achievement, and every generation has to adapt new ways of teaching and learning as technology changes the playing field.

The way people cured ailments, fed themselves, and found entertainment also looks drastically different. Before the modern car trip, dinner could be a longer, slower ritual with multiple courses and elaborate table manners.

Candles and oil lamps lit the evenings, and families gathered around a table for conversations that didn't accumulate a screen time balance. Medicines were a mix of herbal remedies, early chemical concoctions, and a lot of guesswork, with doctors often balancing risk and necessity rather than using precise diagnostics. The idea of "prescription" was more about tradition, family lore, and the doctor's best judgment than about modern lab tests, yet it worked enough to keep communities healthy in many cases.

Layout and travel have changed a lot too. People traveled by horse, wagon, or carriage, and long journeys were considered adventures rather than mere commutes. The concept of a road trip was not as common as it is today, so the idea of spending days in a small car with siblings and parents would have sounded like a challenge and a delight all at once. Roadside stops weren't the same. There weren't the same kinds of fast-food chains or gas stations —part of the journey was the journey itself, with the family stopping for a chat with a neighbor, a taste of a new town's snack, or a quick look at a strange landmark. It was a different pace, a different rhythm, but it was still a way to learn about the world by watching it go by the window.

The games and amusements of everyday life reveal how people stayed curious and kept their minds active without screens. They played marbles, jacks, and games that stretched the imagination and used the items around them. They told stories, shared songs, and built things with hands rather than with apps. A walk in the town square could be a lesson in local history, a chance to spot a building with a story, or a moment to notice how water wheels and windmills turned energy into daily life. The point is simple: the past wasn't a dull, dark place; it was full of clever people who found joy in small things, just like we do when we discover a neat fact on a long car ride.

As the miles roll by, you can help kids see how ordinary rituals shape who we are. Cleanliness, food, language, and play all evolve, sometimes slowly, sometimes with a loud, surprising leap. The way we wash our hands today might seem obvious, but it grew out of centuries of experimentation, habit, and the stubborn belief that small improvements can feel like magic when you're on a road trip and your kids are asking, again, what was life like before the internet. The differences can be fun to compare: a world of chamber pots and candlelight versus a car's cupholders and climate control. The humor is in noticing the contrast and appreciating the resilience and creativity of people who lived before us—and in recognizing that, no matter when we travel, what we want most is to understand the world a little better, together.

5

BIZARRE INVENTIONS THAT ACTUALLY EXISTED

Too-Weird-to-Be-Useful

Some inventions arrive in the world dripping with cleverness and confidence, only to prove that practicality is a different kind of art. They sound brilliant in a boardroom with a whiteboard full of sparkles and megabytes of potential, yet on the road they wobble, slip, or simply refuse to function as advertised. And that's what makes them perfect road-trip fodder. They're not failures so much as conversations waiting to happen, prompts for a quick laugh or a cheeky "Would you actually use that?" test during a long stretch of highway.

Take Pet Rock, for example. It was born in the mid-1970s as a mock-serious joke about consumer culture. A smooth, ordinary rock was placed in a box with a snappy instruction booklet, a pretend backstory, and suddenly the world needed a pet that didn't require feeding or walking. The idea was simple: low maintenance, high humor, and a price tag that felt like a wink. The rock didn't do tricks; it didn't bark or purr. It just existed, and that was the entire charm. People lined up to buy the rocks, fed by the same impulse that makes novelty gifts explode into brief masons of joy around campfires and road stops. The weird thing is not that it existed, but how quickly something so studiously ordinary could become a banner product for a season.

Then there's the Useless Box, a tiny wooden cube with a switch that, once flipped, triggers a tiny mechanism to flip the switch back again. It sounds like a prank played by a mischievous librarian, yet it became a legitimate gadget category. The box promises nothing useful and delivers a pure, gleeful loop of "I did nothing useful, and I'm proud of it." The appeal isn't in solving a problem; it's in the tiny tug of curiosity and the quiet joy of watching a switch work exactly as it shouldn't. It's the kind of device that invites a roomful of people to lean in and say, "One more time," and then another, and another—until a chorus forms about nothing at all but the silliness of cleverness for cleverness's sake.

Selfie Toasters entered the scene with a grin and a crust of toast that looked like a memory. The concept is delightfully silly: a toaster that burns your face onto your breakfast by printing a tiny photo onto the bread. It sounds like a gadget from a tech-obsessed dream world

CRAZY RANDOM FACTS FOR CAR RIDES

driven by social media feeds and morning grumpiness. Yet somewhere between the glossy commercials and the kitchen counter, something real happened. People bought these gadgets, not because they needed to know what their breakfast looked like, but because the moment felt oddly timeless—an absurdity that travels well on road trips where a giggle can be the best fuel for a family's energy.

And then we have the Banana Phone, a curved yellow invention that looks as if it hopped out of a cartoon and into a home gadget catalog. It's not a tool for serious communication; it's a prop for play, a reminder that some tech is more about mood than function. You can answer a call with a banana shape, pretend to speak into a peeler, and share the moment with a chorus of amused passengers. It isn't practical. It isn't supposed to be. It's a celebration of whimsy—the kind of artifact that makes kids tilt their heads and say, "Wait, people paid money for that?" and adults laugh because the answer is yes, they did—and are still doing it in a world that occasionally forgets to laugh.

Why do these things exist? Because road trips are about energy as much as information. They're about the spark that comes from a shared moment of ridiculousness after a long stretch of listening to the engine hum. These inventions prove that you don't need a perfect device to create a memory; you need something to spark curiosity, to invite conversation, to become a part of a family story you'll tell at the next rest stop. They remind us that humor and imagination sometimes outpace utility—and that's a perfectly acceptable kind of usefulness on a long drive.

So as you roll toward the next exit, lean into the silliness. The world is full of weird little inventions that somehow found a way into our lives, if only for a moment or a day. They're not just oddities; they're social experiments, tiny mirrors reflecting our love for novelty, for shared laughter, and for the simple delight of discovering that something can be oddly perfect just the way it is—and that's enough to keep a carful of voices in a chorus of

Accidental Breakthroughs

Some of the greatest tools in modern life began as accidents, happy accidents that looked like dead ends until someone looked a little closer and saw possibility where others saw nothing. The backseat of a car is a great place to learn these stories, because accidents have a way of turning quiet rides into aha moments that keep everyone glancing toward the window and then toward each other with a new kind of curiosity.

The burrs on a Wisconsin walk with his dog gave Georges de Mestral an idea that would become Velcro. He wondered why burrs clung so stubbornly and repeatedly examined their tiny hooks and loops under a microscope. The magic wasn't in a spark of inspiration alone but in patience—the willingness to test and re-test, to improvise, and to keep refining the concept until it could be manufactured. Velcro feel like magic on the surface, a simple pair of words sewn together from two ideas—hook and loop—yet the journey from curiosity to a workday staple took decades. It's a reminder that a small, patient observation can turn into a big, everyday thing that we now use to fasten what matters.

Penicillin came from a chance contamination—an ordinary petri dish in Alexander Fleming's lab that grew mold. The mold happened to kill bacteria all around it, and that dead-brown ring of wonder became a revolution in medicine. At first, Fleming wasn't sure what he'd found, and the world was cautious. But the discovery shifted the course of health forever, letting antibiotics become a cornerstone of modern medicine. It's a story of how a misstep can be the doorway to a future that saves countless lives, a reminder that curiosity needs a little chaos to bloom properly.

The microwave oven arrived when Percy Spencer found a melted chocolate bar in his pocket during a test of radar equipment. A hunch about microwave energy turned into a kitchen revolution. The device that could heat food quickly had to prove itself safe, practical, and actually useful in homes. The path from a lab anomaly to a household staple wasn't overnight, but the leap was real. The microwave carried with it both the promise of convenience and a cautionary note about safety and experimentation. It shows how the most surprising discoveries can arrive as byproducts of curiosity, not as plans in a polished marketing deck.

Post-it Notes began their life as a failed adhesive. A researcher named Spencer Silver created a glue that was too weak for the job it was meant to do. It required a second story, a different kind of thinking, and a creative sparking moment from Arthur Fry, who stuck his bookmark to the page with Silver's glue and realized it could cling without leaving a mess. The product was refined, marketed, and ultimately found a surprising home on every desk in the world. It's a gentle reminder that some of the best fixes aren't about stronger glue but about a smarter approach to reuse and flexibility. These stories—Velcro, penicillin, the microwave, Post-it Notes—don't share a single blueprint for success. They share a common thread: the willingness to follow a stray idea until it reveals its own usefulness, often in places you never expected.

Road trips invite you to notice those moments. They're not always dramatic; sometimes they arrive as tiny, almost inaudible hints—an odd result in a lab, a chance observation on a dusty shelf, a clumsy mistake that becomes essential. The next time you hear a disclaimer about "accidents," remember that some of the world's most useful inventions started with one or two wrong turns, then stayed long enough to become right for millions of people. The car's engine hum becomes a metronome for patience, the seat becomes a front-row seat to history, and the shared laughter between fuel stops becomes the chorus that carries an idea from a napkin sketch to a household name.

Fashion Fails and Gadgets

Not every invention is a sustenance for progress; some are fashion statements that forgot to wear practicality well. In the backseat, these clever misfires become instant conversation starters. They're the kind of designs that make you pause, squint, and imagine what the creator's desk looked like—maybe a little like a carnival, maybe a little like a science fair with sparks and sequins. And yet they matter. They stand as evidence that the boundary between whimsy and usefulness is, at times, thinner than a thread held together by ambition and a dash of whimsy.

Mood rings are a classic example. They shimmered their way onto fingers in the 1970s with bold, rainbow hues that were supposed to reveal inner moods by the way you felt. The science behind the magic was more about temperature than emotion. The ring's colors changed with the body's heat and mood, or so the marketing claimed. People wore them with an earnest belief in a romance of self-understanding, then laughed when the color suggested emotions they'd rather keep private. It wasn't a failure so much as a cultural capsule—a tiny, sparkly indicator of how fashion can ride a scientific fad into the uncanny. Mood rings remind us that the road trip is half fashion, half science show, and wholly a stage for people to express themselves in in-between moments of traffic and sun glare.

Umbrella hats have a more literal take on the same idea. They bring together function and theater, a hat that carries its own rain shield. The concept isn't bad in theory—hands-free protection in a sudden downpour is a dream for travelers who hate juggling umbrellas. In practice, most people look slightly ridiculous wearing a swinging canopy atop their head, and the wind has a way of turning such a gadget into a prop for comedy. Yet the umbrella hat survives as a carnival favorite, a reminder that some inventions exist precisely because someone said, "What if…?" and someone else said, "Let's try it." There's a communal humor in watching someone stride confidently through a drizzle with a hat umbrella that looks like it could deploy a parachute if the weather demanded it.

Propeller beanies were another splash of goofy innovation. The spinning propeller on top of a cap was a quintessential symbol of late-90s gadget culture, a visual pun that shouted, "I'm tech-adjacent and proudly silly." They had a moment when teen fashion and novelty tech collided, and the result was more about the memory of the moment than about longevity or efficiency. The propeller beanie teaches an important lesson: some items exist to mark a trend and then fade, leaving behind stories that keep the road alive with laughter and the photo albums with goofy portraits. Google Glass represents a more modern wearable misstep. It promised a future where information rides on a transparent headset, but privacy concerns, injuries of social etiquette, and the awkwardness of wearing a computer on your face quickly turned it into a cautionary tale. It exists in memory as a symbol of brave experimentation that didn't fully land—yet it still spurred wealth of discussion about how we might wear technology without losing human connection.

Finally, even everyday fashion gadgets like LED sneakers and mood-enhanced jewelry remind us that style and function don't always co-author the moment. LED sneakers were the dream of glowing streets and confident entrances, and they still show up at occasional fashion shows or retro parties. Mood jewelry, with its shimmering stones that hinted at emotion, became a cottage industry for people who love to decorate their moods in public. The magic lies not in their staying power but in how they shifted the way we talk about ourselves on the move. If a road trip is a stage, then these gadgets are the costumes, allowing everyone to play along, to laugh, and to appreciate that sometimes the most memorable technology is the one that makes a moment feel a little more theatrical, a little more like a performance rather than a reliable tool.

The "Why Did Nobody Buy This?" Test

This final corner of the chapter is a playful exercise in curiosity. It's a quick game you can play with the car rolling down the highway, a guessing game about which odd products actually existed and which were simply clever fantasies assembled for a joke on a rainy afternoon. Imagine four items sliding into the backseat as you drive: a banana-shaped phone that actually functioned as a Bluetooth handset, a self-stirring mug that could whisk your coffee to a perfect swirl with the press of a button, a practical yet almost impossible to use umbrella hat that promised hands-free rain protection, and a mysterious demo piece that claimed to be the world's first mood-aware belt buckle.

The banana-shaped phone is real. It wasn't just a gag; it found a niche in novelty stores and gift catalogs, and it still makes people smile when they spot it in a kid's backpack or a novelty desk. The self-stirring mug is also real. It uses a tiny motor to keep beverages circulating, a quirky marvel of miniaturization that somehow felt both clever and ridiculous at the same time. The umbrella hat genuinely exists, a wearable that brings rain protection to a new level of theatrical efficiency and comic value. The mood-aware belt buckle, however, is a fictional addition to this quartet, a joke product that relies on the romance of a mood-detecting accessory without any real-world system to do the mood sensing.

Which ones did you think were real? If you guessed that all four were real, you'll be surprised to learn that one of them was a clever fabrication—the mood-aware belt buckle was never produced for mass sale. It's a reminder that the road to discovery often includes detours into the realm of whimsy, where some ideas never quite leave the sketchbook but still spark imagination. If you want a more rigorous version of this game, you can add more items and a quick check after each ride—have the family guess whether an invention existed or was a playful invention of the moment. The point isn't correctness; it's curiosity. It's about teaching kids to ask questions, to follow a thread, and to enjoy the moment of discovery together. In a car ride, this becomes a tiny, portable science fair—one that travels with you, and one that leaves you with four stories to tell at the next rest stop.

6

FOOD FACTS THAT FEEL LIKE PRANKS

Foods That Used to Be Different

Food does not stay still. It follows people, trade routes, and clever cooks who reinvent what counts as a snack, a staple, or a celebration dish. On a road trip, you might reach for a bag of chips and a bottle of water, and in your mind you could be tasting a history lesson that happened centuries ago. The changes are often small, but the effect is big. A tomato today is almost a cliche of everyday life. But there was a time when tomatoes were not just unfamiliar, they were considered a danger to eat. In parts of Europe, tomatoes were grown and admired as ornamental fruit, their bright red skins brightening gardens more than kitchens. People believed they could cause disease; the plant's glossy look was enough to make folks cautious. It took a long, curious stretch of trial and taste testing before tomatoes became a pantry staple in families, on pizzas, and in sauces across the world. The journey from ornamental curiosity to everyday food is a reminder that perception can be as influential as the food itself.

Chocolate is another reliable road companion that hides a surprising backstory. The bitter beverage of the ancient Maya and Aztec civilizations traveled a long road to become the sweet treat we crave today. The cocoa bean was roasted, ground, and mixed with water, chile, and sometimes vanilla—an exotic drink that could be ceremonial, even sacred. When Europeans tasted cocoa in the Age of Exploration, they added sugar and milk, turning it into a smooth, dessert-like experience. The idea of chocolate as a candy bar or milk chocolate is only a relatively recent shift in a story that began as a bitter, spicy drink. On a ride, you can imagine those ancient cups clinking while someone in the backseat asks, with a grin, whether the chocolate we love now would still taste good if you forgot the sugar.

Color matters in the kitchen, too. Carrots did not always arrive in that perfect, uniform orange. Before modern breeding, many varieties existed in purple, white, and yellow hues. It wasn't until farmers in the Netherlands selected certain traits and kept nurturing them that the bright orange carrot became the new normal. That small steering of nature, a century-long effort, changed what people expect to see on the plate and in the soup. When you spot an orange carrot in a lunchbox, you're seeing a trace of history—an example of how a simple color change can become a universal standard.

Ice cream is a chilly reminder that technology shapes flavor. Long before refrigerators and freezers, people dreamed of cold desserts. In ancient China and in medieval Persia, people used ice and snow mixed with fruit and milk to cool treats down, often turning them into luxury indulgences for the wealthy. By the time sugar and cream joined the party in Europe, and by the era of hand-cranked churns, ice cream started to resemble the modern scoops we crave on sunny road stops. Each bite is a blend of ancient longing and modern convenience—the perfect symbol for a road trip snack that feels like a time machine with a freezer.

Popcorn has been popping its sparkly little kernels for longer than many travelers have known how to navigate a car's map system. The oldest evidence of popcorn shows up in ancient structures in the Americas, where people popped corn to make a fun, easy-to-store treat. Unlike many snacks that require ovens or schedules, popcorn is practically made for a car ride: a few kernels in a bag, a quick heat, and a burst of tiny white stars that light up the fingers and the storybook in your mind. The fact that popcorn has persevered from ancient kernels to movie theaters shows how sometimes the simplest technique—heat plus a little pressure—produces a memory that travels with you wherever you go.

Finally, think about white bread and the rise of refined sugar in everyday meals. For generations, many households baked bread with the whole grain and the crust intact. White bread, meanwhile, emerged as bakers refined flour, removing parts of the grain to create a softer, lighter slice. Sugar followed a parallel path: once a luxury, it became a staple that sweetened far more than just desserts. These shifts did not erase old flavors; they layered new experiences on top of them, changing not just how food tastes but how families organize their kitchens, budgets, and celebrations. On a car ride, you can reflect on how each of these changes reflects the dynamics of culture, technology, and taste—and how many of today's favorites might be seen as curious echoes of yesterday's experiments.

The big takeaway is simple: foods reshape themselves as people, environments, and habits change. Nothing is fixed forever, and every bite might be carrying a secret about the past. As you munch or sip, you're participating in a long conversation about what humans value in flavor, texture, and memory. What other foods do you think used to be different, just waiting for a curious cook to rewrite their story? That playful idea keeps a drive from ever getting dull: curiosity, served warm with a side of laughter.

Strange Ingredients, Real Meals

The world serves up meals that read like a choose-your-own-adventure in a grocery store. Some ingredients arrive in our kitchens through centuries of cultural exchange, while others come from the bold experiments of modern food science. The result is a pantry full of surprises that can spark conversation, debate, and giggles on a long ride. If you're ever in doubt about trying something new, remember: many foods that sound strange at first become favorites once you hear the story behind them.

Insects as everyday fare might sound like a dare, but they're a practical and increasingly popular source of protein in many parts of the world. Roasted crickets or fried mealworms are crunchy, light, and surprisingly satisfying to those who grew up with them. They're often seasoned with salt, lime, or chili to mimic familiar flavors, and their tiny size makes them easy to share in a car with friends who love a quick challenge. The idea that protein can come from something the size of a peppercorn is an invitation to rethink the usual suspects in our snack bags. It's also a gentle reminder that flavor culture is not a fixed map—it's a living, tasting experiment that travels with travelers.

Huitlacoche, sometimes called corn smut, is another rare traveler that has found a home on plates far from its origin. In Mexican cooking, this fungus swells kernels into a rich, mushroom-like delicacy. People savor its earthy aroma and nutty sweetness, a flavor profile that could remind you of truffle but with a distinct corn backdrop. Eating huitlacoche is a friendly reminder that what a culture considers edible is not universal. A car's windows might be rolled down, the scent could drift into the car, and someone could say, "What's that wonderful aroma?" Only to be answered with a delighted smile: it's history, soil, and a little fungus, all in one bite.

Century eggs, or preserve-eggs, are another striking example of how preservation can transform flavor and color. A pale green yolk surrounded by a resinous, blackish-white jelly might sound odd, but it's a beloved delicacy in parts of Asia. The green yolk offers a creamy, almost sulfurous richness that pairs with rice or congee, turning a simple breakfast into a ritual. The way centuries of curing, salt, and time transform a plain egg into something so bold demonstrates how technique is cuisine's secret ingredient. When a traveler bites into a century egg, they're tasting an old method that still has a place at modern tables.

Natto is a fermented soybean dish that stretches the imagination in both aroma and texture. The beans are sticky, stringy, and have a powerful nutty scent that some find challenging, others irresistible. In Japan, natto is often served with soy sauce, mustard, and sometimes scallions, a breakfast staple that invites you to savor patience and tradition. The way natto benefits from fermentation is a gentler, more accessible version of chemistry at work in your hands. It demonstrates that flavor sometimes comes from the most unlikely corners of the kitchen—where bacteria do the heavy lifting and tradition dictates the final bite.

Stinky tofu is another fermented wonder that can trigger a sensory roller coaster. In Taiwan and parts of Southeast Asia, this tofu is soaked, fermented, and fried, giving it a pungent aroma that can surprise first-timers. Yet many fans describe it as silky, creamy, and deeply comforting once it hits the mouth. It's a vivid example of how scent and taste stand in dynamic tension, how a strong initial impression can yield a creamy, mellow finish. If you test it on a road trip, you'll likely hear questions ranging from curiosity to comedic disbelief—right before laughter takes over.

Fermented shark, or hakarl, is a cautionary tale about tradition meeting daring curiosity. In Iceland, small volumes of shark meat are cured and hung to dry for months. The smell is so strong that many visitors describe it as ammonia-like. Despite its intensity, some people adore hakarl for the unique, briny, almost peppery taste that emerges after the initial punch. Hakarl is a reminder that food culture often honors extremes— whether in texture, aroma, or patience. It's not something you're likely to see in a grocery store; it's the kind of culinary dare that becomes a memorable story during a long ride.

If there's a universal verdict in this section, it's this: location does not determine value so much as context does. What sounds strange in one kitchen might be cherished in another, especially when it comes with a story. Consider durian, the fruit with a reputation that precedes it. Some people call its aroma intoxicating, while others describe it as unappealingly strong. But when the same fruit is tasted in a different setting, many discover a custardy, almost almond-like sweetness tucked behind that notorious smell. For a car ride, the moral is playful: keep an open mind and listen to the tale as much as the taste.

The list would be incomplete without a nod to edible organisms that your grandparents might have told you were insects in disguise—the edible kinds, that is. Escamoles, the prized ant larvae of Mexico, offer a delicate nuttiness in many preparations, a reminder that tiny things can carry big flavors. Haggis, in its own way, bridges cultures by combining organ meats with spices and oatmeal into a single, compact patty that tells a story of history, scarcity, and ingenuity. Each bite invites a conversation about whether the flavor world has more room for curiosity than fear. And that is the heart of this section: real meals sometimes come from ideas that once sounded like a dare, and the dare can lead to an enduring taste memory.

Surprise Science in Your Snack

What makes a snack feel magical, almost like a tiny science experiment you can taste? The answer is a mix of chemistry, physics, and the simple joy of watching ordinary things transform under the right conditions. On a road trip, you can turn any bite into a mini science lesson that's easy to enjoy and even easier to repeat.

Take caramelization and the Maillard reaction, two kitchen chemistries that give color and flavor to many snacks. Caramelization happens when the natural sugars in foods heat up and break apart, turning from pale to a deep amber and then to a rich, toasty taste. It's behind the glossy surface of caramel and the browned edges on roasted nuts. The Maillard reaction is a cousin of caramelization, but it involves the interaction of amino acids and sugars during browning. It creates that warm, roasted, savory note you smell when a burger browns in a pan. These reactions are why toasting bread or searing meat makes everything taste more alive. It's not magic; it's molecules rearranging themselves under heat, giving you a more complex bite with every turn of the wheel.

Emulsions are another everyday act of culinary chemistry. Mayonnaise, hollandaise, and even mustard rely on emulsification, where tiny droplets of fat are kept suspended in water-based liquids by an emulsifier like egg yolk or mustard seeds. When you drizzle oil into a bowl and whisk, the mixture goes from sleek to silky as the oil disperses into tiny droplets that don't separate out. That moment when your sauce holds together is a tiny victory of science you can taste, and it makes a simple sandwich feel like a chef's creation.

Fizz and bubbles are the punctuation marks of drinks. Soda pop comes from dissolved carbon dioxide under pressure. Open a bottle and the gas escapes, forming bubbles that dance in the liquid. That fizz is not just for show; it's carbonation, a reminder of how pressure and temperature work in tandem. If you've ever wondered why sparkling drinks feel lighter on the tongue, you've witnessed a physics trick—gas under pressure behaving differently when released. The science is so neat that some people collect micro-bubbles in cold beverages as if they're little time capsules of the cellars and caves that first brewed them.

Fermentation deserves special attention here because it's the oldest kitchen science. Yeast turning sugar into alcohol and carbon dioxide is a tiny factory with a big payoff. Bread rises as gas from fermentation expands the dough, creating those porous, chewy interiors we associate with a good loaf. Yogurt gains its tang from lactic acid produced by bacteria, which also helps preserve it. Fermentation changes not just texture and flavor but how long something stays edible. It's a natural, slow chemistry project that people have been doing for ages, turning simple ingredients in their cupboards into reliable staples.

Gelation, the science of turning liquids into gels, is another everyday magic trick. Puddings, yogurts, jelly jams, and even some candies rely on gelatin, pectin, or other thickening agents to set. When you pour liquid into a mold and wait, you're giving long chains of molecules time to lace together, forming a network that traps liquid and holds shape. The result is a dessert you can slice and share, with a texture that feels almost like a edible sculpture. It's science in a spoonful, a reminder that patience in the kitchen can yield structure as well as flavor.

Then there's temperature and flavor. Temperature changes how we perceive sweetness, saltiness, and even bitterness. A cold scoop of ice cream can taste sweeter than the same scoop at room temperature because our taste buds respond to temperature as it changes our mouth's chemistry. Ice in a soda or a cool bite of fruit can crisp the palate and reset the taste buds for the next mouthful. When you're on a road trip, you can play with temperature by letting a warm snack cool on your tongue and then contrasting it with a cold drink. The difference isn't just sensation; it's a demonstration of how context shapes flavor.

Flavor is also carried by texture. A smooth chocolate bar feels different from a crunchy nut square, even if the core flavor is similar. The mouthfeel is a kind of chemistry, where fat, air, and delicate crystals work together to create a sensation that makes the same substance feel new.

Texture can be the final clue to a snack's identity, and science helps explain why one bite feels exciting while another feels ordinary.

Last, let's give a nod to the science of freshness. Enzymes in fruit can break down cell walls, releasing aromas that tell you the fruit is ripening. But if you slow or stop that process with chilling or preservation, you can extend a snack's life and keep it tasting crisp longer. That's why cherries stay bright in a jar and tomatoes keep their snap on a long car ride. The science of freshness translates directly into how we plan snacks for long trips, how we store them, and how we negotiate with ourselves about when to eat them.

In short, snacks are more than taste. They're a daily micro-lab where heat, air, water, fat, and time do a careful dance. The next time you bite into something you enjoy, pause long enough to notice the texture, the aroma, and the tiny science behind it. You'll likely find that curiosity is as irresistible as the flavor itself, and you'll have a natural excuse to share the science story with your travel companions.

Gross-Sounding, Delicious Results

Some foods arrive with names that sound like a dare, and then surprise you by being delicious enough to change the entire mood of a road trip. The trick is to keep the tone light, know that taste is personal, and allow the dare to lead to a conversation rather than a scare. When you hear a word that makes you go "eww," lean into the story behind it and give your palate a chance to catch up with your curiosity.

Rocky Mountain oysters are a classic example. The name suggests something marine, perhaps a fancy sea creature, but this snack is a dish of fried bull testicles. The idea may sound bold or even silly, but for many who grew up with it, the texture is crisp and the flavor surprisingly mild. It's a reminder that a name can be louder than the bite, and that some foods are loved precisely because they push people outside their comfort zone. If you approach it as a story rather than a dare, you can turn a moment of hesitation into a moment of laughter and learning.

Haggis is another example of how history can shape a plate. The idea of cooking an organ-meat mixture inside a sheep's stomach might sound odd, yet the result is a hearty, comforting dish in many parts of the world. The sensory shock of the first bite fades as the spices and grains soften the texture and reveal a deep, savory finish. On a road trip, a haggis moment becomes a conversation about culture and ingenuity, and that conversation is often the best kind of snack companion you can have.

Casu marzu, a cheese famous for its maggots, ranks high on the scale of gross-sounding foods. It's a rarity, a dare, and a culinary risk that only a few daring eaters seek out. The maggots help ferment the cheese further, producing a creamy, almost piquant finish for the bravest palates. If you're curious enough to explore, remember that it's not for everyone, and that its reputation is as much about the story of Sardinian cheesemaking as about taste itself. To curious travelers, it's a reminder that extreme flavors belong to cultures that celebrate boldness in the kitchen.

Stinky tofu is a standout for its bold aroma. Fermented and fried, this tofu throws a scent bomb that can surprise first-timers. Yet once you take that first bite, many discover a soft, creamy interior with a gentle, savory umami. The initial reaction is often laughter, followed by appreciation, as the funk becomes an accompaniment to a comforting, well-seasoned bite. It's a perfect example of how a strong start can lead to a surprising, satisfying finish when you're open to the ride.

Durian is famous or infamous for its smell, depending on who you ask. Some travelers avoid it at all costs; others swear by its custardy sweetness, a blend that resembles almonds and cream with a hint of tropical warmth. The outward reputation of durian is loud, but the taste can be delicate and luxurious once you get past the first impression. It's a reminder that in food, as in travel, appearances can be a trick. The real treasure often lies beyond the first sniff or the first bite, waiting for someone willing to look past the surface.

Escamoles, the delicate ant larvae from Mexico, may sound like a dare but carry a buttery, nutty note that many eat with warm tortillas or in a light salsa. The idea of eating insect larvae may feel odd to some, yet escamoles demonstrate that texture and flavor can exist at the edge of expectation. It's not about shock value; it's about the surprising alignment between a tiny organism and a big, satisfying taste.

What these foods teach us is simple: sometimes the strangest-sounding dish yields the most comforting bite when the setting, the culture, and the moment come together. On a road trip, a "gross" food can become a gateway to laughter, to a story you'll tell later, and to a sense of connection with people who eat differently. The punchline is that curiosity often tastes better than fear, and a good story makes the bite feel even bigger. So next time a name makes you pause, take a breath, lean in, and let the flavor lead the way.

7

EARTH IS A WEIRD PLANET (UNDERSTATEMENT)

Places That Don't Look Real

The ground beneath your tires isn't just dirt and grass and asphalt. It's a stage for nature's best photo editor, reshaping itself into landscapes that look like they were dropped into the world from a dream or a science-fiction wallpaper. As you drive, keep an eye out not just for the road but for the window-sized panoramas that seem to have been stretched, bent, or retouched by some mischievous geologist with a knack for magic. These are places that look photoshopped in real life, and yet they're very much 100% real.

Take Salar de Uyuni in Bolivia, the world's largest salt flat. When a shallow layer of water covers the plain after rain, the surface shivers into a perfect mirror that reflects the sky, the clouds, and the horizon until you can't tell where the road ends and the air begins. It's like driving through a map that's been washed clean and then pressed flat onto the ground. In the right light, you can stand on a slab of salt with nothing but air between your feet and the clouds, a goofy juxtaposition that turns every mile into a tall tale you'll want to tell again and again.

Then there's Antelope Canyon in Arizona, a slot canyon carved step by patient step by water and wind. The walls lean in close, their sandstone curves catching sunlight that filters down in laser-streaks. When the sun is high, you see vertical pencils of light that look ready-made for a movie poster. It's nature's answer to a glass sculpture—soft, sculpted curves and a glow that makes you squint and smile at the same time.

Pamukkale in Turkey offers a different kind of unreal: chalk-white terraces that look like frozen waterfalls, but they're formed by warm mineral springs dripping limestone over thousands of years. The surface is so bright you almost need sunglasses, and the effect on your sense of scale is wild. You can step onto a tiered pool and feel like you've accidentally wandered into a candy-coated dream; the water is warm, the rocks are chalky, and the whole scene seems to glow from within.

In China, the Zhangye Danxia landform creates mountains painted in stripes of red, yellow, green, and blue—layers that look as if the earth wore a vertical rainbow like a badge of honor. The colors aren't sprayed by a painter; they're the result of minerals in the rocks and long, slow weathering. The result is a panorama that keeps changing with your angle of view, a living postcard you can drive toward but never quite catch.

The Marble Caves, tucked in General Carrera Lake on the border of Chile and Argentina, are another kind of optical trick. The river's turquoise waters nibble away at limestone, sculpting caves whose walls curve into smooth, glossy contours. The water's glassy surface turns the caverns into a pair of underwater mirrors—if you lean in, you might swear you see the outside world staged behind you.

Then there are Cappadocia's fairy chimneys in Turkey, spires of rock that have stood guard over valleys since long before photography existed. Winds hollowed soft volcanic ash into towers, and people built homes, churches, and even whole cities inside them. From above, they look like a hoard of mushroom-shaped towers; from the ground, you step into a landscape that feels like a whimsy you could reach out and touch.

No visit to these places is complete without letting curiosity drift into a game: what if this was a painting, and what if the painter forgot to turn off nature's signature engine? The reality is that the world is a better photo editor than any software, and the window between reality and fantasy is thinner than you think. Look for the tiny tells—the way light dances on a slick rock surface, the way a canyon narrows just when your laughter begins to echo, the way a shallow pool catches a sky you recognize but can't quite place. These aren't tricks; they're Earth's way of showing off its backstage pass.

As you point out the window, ask questions that turn the ride into a mini-museum tour. How did this place form? What would it look like from the air? If you took a photo here and edited it to exaggerate the colors, would anyone notice? These moments are perfect for a backseat scavenger hunt: spot the natural feature that seems too perfect, or imagine you're guiding a postcard tour through the world's most convincing illusions. And if you're a kid who loves stories, share a legend about the place—the ancient myths that often attach themselves to landscapes that look like they're from another planet. The ground isn't just land; it's a library of pictures waiting to be read aloud in the car.

What makes these places especially friendly for road trips is their potential for quick, vivid storytelling. You don't need to memorize dates or scientific names to enjoy them. A few vivid verbs—glow, tilt, ripple, melt, bend—can carry you across continents without a single map coordinate. The goal isn't to lecture; it's to spark a shared sense of wonder. The road is your classroom, the scenery your teacher, and the window a portal that turns every mile into a story you'll retell at the dinner table with extra giggles.

And remember, you don't have to go far to find this kind of magic. Even a pass-through on a weekend road trip—an overlook that makes the landscape look unreal, a cliff-fed river cutting a silver arc through rock, a field of striped hills—can become a stand-in for a legendary destination. The Earth is full of these "Are we sure this isn't CGI?" moments, and every one of them is another chance to turn a routine drive into a burst of curiosity and laughter.

Weather That Breaks the Rules

When the sky grabs the spotlight, it often does things that feel almost mischievous. Weather, at its boldest, doesn't just threaten rain; it flirtates with possibility. It makes the familiar feel fantastical, and that's perfect for turning a long drive into a wonder show. This section is about storms and temperatures that seem to ignore the rules, dazzling with color, sound, and surprise.

Catatumbo lightning, a thunderstorm that hovers over Lake Maracaibo in Venezuela for hours on end, is a natural light show that blurs the line between weather and wizardry. You can imagine the night sky turning into a slow, electric choir, with bolts flashing again and again as if the weather itself were clapping its hands. The phenomenon is famous not just for its intensity but for its persistence, lighting up the horizon like a neon sign for nature's own electricity festival. It's not dangerous in the way a tornado is, but it is serious in its insistence that the atmosphere loves drama.

Then there are the more intimate fire-themed cousins of weather: fire whirls, or fire tornadoes, born when a wildfire's heat and a swirl of wind meet. They're not common, but when they occur they behave like the planet's most unpredictable dares. A twisting column of flame acts like a living vortex, scouring the ground and painting the air with smoke and heat. For drivers, imagining a fire whirl is a reminder that wind can be as much a player as the flame itself—an atmosphere with a sense of mischief, swirling in unpredictable patterns.

Ball lightning is the kind of rumor you tell at a sleepover and immediately realize you want to see for yourself. This glowing sphere, occasionally the size of a softball or a basketball, seems to float through the air during storms. It's rare enough that many scientists treat it as a legend until they catch a glimpse. If you ever see one—a bright, hovering ball that doesn't quite obey gravity—you'll remember a car ride where science felt like a magic trick and quietly decide you'll be a better weather watcher on the next turn.

Thundersnow and other heavy-snow storms are not your average winter weather. Thunder is loud enough to shake cups on the dashboard, even as snow falls in a way that muffles the world into a whispering white. It's a reminder that weather has a sense of theater: the thunder roars like a crowd, while the snow softens like a quilt. Thundersnow lets kids pretend they're inside a snow globe that's been shaken just a little too vigorously.

Blood rain is a term that sounds straight out of a fantasy novel, but it has shown up in real places. Red-tinted rain often traces back to microscopic spores or dust carried aloft by storms, coloring rain as it falls. In other times and places, places have witnessed rain tinted by iron-rich dust or volcanic ash. The sight can be startling and a little eerie, yet it's a vivid reminder that even something as routine as rain can arrive wearing a strange, almost cinematic hue.

Colder-than-expected surprises aren't limited to red rain. We've seen frost that doesn't quite belong on a calendar, fog that clings to windows like a translucent curtain, and temperatures that swing wildly from extremes in a single day. It's the kind of weather that makes you reach for a coat you didn't know you needed and then glance at the sky with a grin, as if to remind the world that normal is just a suggestion.

For kids and grown-ups alike, the magic of these unusual weather events lies not in fear but in curiosity. What causes lightning to appear in a calm night? How can rain arrive tinted with color or snow fall with a thunderous chorus? The answers are intricate and fascinating, yet the questions are easy: what would you wear to stay comfy during a night when the sky puts on a light show? What would you name a weather event you saw in your own city? These questions invite conversation during car rides, making weather feel like a science fair with every turn of the wheel.

And a practical note for road trips: when you're in the thick of a dramatic weather moment, point out the phenomenon, describe it briefly, and shift to a quick game. Quick sketches on a napkin of what's happening can be surprisingly engaging. The idea isn't to overwhelm with terms but to let everyone feel like an explorer in motion, learning something new with every mile.

Upshots of extreme weather are not just entertainment; they're a doorway into science that's visible, tactile, and, best of all, shareable. The car becomes a cozy classroom where the sky is the professor and the road is the chalkboard. You don't need a lab or a conference room to enjoy the surprise and awe that come with weather that breaks the rules.

Rocks, Crystals, and Hidden Treasure

Earth doesn't just throw rocks at you; it curates them with dramatic flair, placing gems and curios in places you'd never expect. Rocks become stories, crystals become weather vanes for the planet's mood, and natural treasures wait to be discovered beneath cliffs and inside caves. In this section we'll walk through some of the planet's most dazzling mineral tales—the kind that spark questions, yield jaw-dropping photos, and quietly become the family's next favorite scavenger-hunt topic.

A good starting point is the Naica Crystal Cave in Chihuahua, Mexico, a place famous for crystals so large that explorers could drive a car or disappear into their shade. The room is cavernous and hot, a reminder that some of nature's best wonders come with a big temperature warning. The crystals here—clear, pale blue, and as long as people are tall—grew in a mineral bath that cooled very slowly over millions of years. It's not a playground for casual curiosity; it's a reminder that Earth's patience is measured in millennia, not minutes. But for a story in a car ride, it's perfect: imagine crystal chandeliers the size of a school gym, glimmering as if the rock itself learned how to glitter.

Geodes, those perfectly plain rocks on the outside that hold a secret world on the inside, offer a second kind of treasure. When you crack one open, you might find a glittering greenhouse of crystals—often quartz, amethyst, or agate—arranged like tiny cathedral windows. The surprise is always in the contrast: a rough, dusty exterior giving way to a breathtaking interior that looks like the inside of a treasure chest. It's geology with a wink, a reminder that beauty can hide in plain sight and that a tiny crack can reveal a universe inside a rock.

Obsidian is Earth's black glass, a rock that forms when lava cools so quickly that crystals don't have time to form. It's as if the ground whispered, "Let's try something sleek," and created a glossy, razor-sharp natural material. Obsidian often marks the edge of civilizations as well, since ancient peoples used it for tools and weapons because it could be chipped to a sharp, fine edge. Today it's a gorgeous fossil of volcanic behavior: glass formed by heat, shaped by time, and polished by countless hands across generations. A rock with a memory and a shine that begs to be touched.

Pumice is a light, fluffy rock that can float, carried on wind and rivers as if it were a cloud that decided to take a vacation on land. Touch a piece and you'll feel it's lighter than air but sturdy enough to survive a long run in a river. It's formed when gas bubbles get trapped in lava as it erupts, and the bubbles pop, leaving behind a millions-of-years-old foam that's turned into floating stone. Pumice isn't just a curiosity; it's a reminder that Earth crafts things that defy everyday expectations, turning the mundane into the playful wonderland of a rock that can ride the surface of water like a tiny, airborne boat.

Crystals within caves aren't always as dramatic as Naica's giants, but they are no less fascinating. Stalactites and stalagmites grow like slow-ticking clockwork, stretching down from the ceiling and rising up from the floor as mineral-rich water drips and evaporates. The textures and shapes tell centuries of stories in a single snapshot. In some places, you'll find selenite crystals that glow with their own pale light, turning cave walls into a quiet stage for a kind of mineral magic. The lesson is simple: Earth stores memories in mineral form, and a quiet crack or a slow drip can turn a rock into a memory keeper.

Hidden treasures aren't always in caves. Rivers and deserts scatter golds and colorful minerals in their beds, forming patterns that look like natural art. Placer deposits —sand and gravel carrying a heavy load of gold, sapphires, or tiny crystals—invite curious scavengers to spot a glint and follow it with eyes that light up like a treasure map. The real treasure is not the metal or gem alone but the sense of possibility—the idea that something marvelous can hide in plain sight, waiting to be found by a traveler who decides to slow down and look a bit closer.

And if you're a kid who loves a treasure-hunting game, you can turn any detour into a small expedition. Look for rocks that feel unusually smooth or heavy, or pockets of glittery dust in a riverbed that might be a clue. Bring a compact magnifying glass or a shell to compare textures and colors. The backseat becomes a tiny field laboratory where each rock tells a tiny story and every pebble could be the key to the next great question. The world's minerals are a vast encyclopedia that you can literally hold in your hand, and that makes every road trip a potential gem-hunting trip.

The real magic of rocks and crystals is how they connect to the rest of the Earth's stories. A cave's crystal can show us the planet's past while a river's gold dust hints at the slow, patient work of erosion. A glassy obsidian surface wonders aloud about volcanic events and the heat that once danced across the landscape. It's a reminder that the ground hides epic tales beneath its surface, stories that speak to curious minds with the quiet, steady voice of rock and mineral turning over in the hands of time.

Natural "Lights" and "Booms"

The night sky, the sea, the forest floor—these places aren't silent. They're full of natural light and resounding sounds that aren't wasting energy. When you drive at dusk or near a coastline, you're traveling through a living light show and a chorus of natural booms. The trick is to listen with your eyes and look with your ears, turning the car into a sort of moving planetarium where each stoplight becomes a mini-museum spotlight for Earth's spectacles.

Aurora borealis and aurora australis, the northern and southern lights, are celestial dancers. They glow in greens and purples, swirling over high latitudes as charged particles from the sun collide with Earth's atmosphere. It's a show that loves darkness and patience, the kind of phenomenon that rewards travelers who keep their schedules flexible and their curiosity open. If you catch a green shimmer bending across the sky, you'll know you've stumbled into a moment many people only read about in books. The science is accessible: solar wind hits our atmosphere, excites oxygen and nitrogen, and the result is a shimmering curtain that can make a night ride feel magical.

Noctilucent clouds, those twinkling high-altitude wisps, ride near the edge of space and drift across twilight skies. They're lit by the Sun long after it has set for those low on the ground, a reminder that Earth has layers not visible until you tilt your head just right. Spotting them is a subtle thrill, the kind of moment that can inspire a pause in the driving and a quick "Let's look at the sky for a minute."

Bioluminescent beings bring the sea and the shore to life in the most literal sense. In places like Mosquito Bay in Puerto Rico or certain coastal beaches around Iceland and California, waves glow with a blue-green light whenever they're disrupted. When a foot lands in the water or a paddle stirs the surface, little creatures beneath the glowwort respond with a gentle spark. It's not a neon sign; it's a quiet chemical glow that makes the ocean seem to glow from within, a reminder that life finds a way to light up even the darkest nights.

Glowworms, too, offer a softer, ground-level light show. In caves where larvae hang silk threads like strings of tiny lanterns, the entire ceiling becomes a starry night under a rock roof. Bats might drift past and the air may smell of damp earth, but what you notice is the soft blue shimmer winding down the walls. It's a gentle version of Earth's light show that invites a hushed, curious moment rather than a loud celebration.

From the heavens, we also get light in more dramatic ways: the green flash at sunset, a brief moment when the sun's edge clips the horizon and a green line briefly presses across the sky. It lasts mere seconds, but it's exactly the kind of moment you want to call out to your car companions, turning the end of a sunny day into a shared, almost whispered, spectacle.

Light isn't the only star in the show. Booms come in many tones and stories as well. The sonic shock of a meteor—when a space rock blazes through the atmosphere—sends a traveling boom that can be heard far from the point of entry. You won't see it and hear it at the same moment, but the memory of a distant flash followed by a rolling thunderclap is enough to spark a quick discussion about space rocks, atmospheric friction, and how far sound travels through air.

The "booms" of Earth aren't always spectacular in scale. Deserts host the haunting, near-silent music of wind across dunes, until suddenly a gust lifts the sand and creates the sound people call "singing sands." It's a gentle, rolling boom in a way—soft, deep, and almost musical—as if the desert itself were tapping its hidden toes. Thunder that rumbles across a valley, rain that hammers a roof, even the crack of a boulder breaking free in a mountainside—these are all the Earth's way of announcing its presence, a reminder that the planet isn't quiet when we're not listening.

And it doesn't stop at light and sound. The natural world loves a surprise so much that it often pairs them: a bird wing catching a glow-worm-lit cave, a bioluminescent wave pulsing with silvery light as it breaks on the shore, or a storm lighting the sky with a flicker of color before the rain arrives. These moments make road trips feel like adventures that didn't need a map—moments that you'll remember because they hooked your kids' curiosity and prompted questions you wouldn't have thought to ask.

To make the most of these experiences, invite conversation. Name the colors you see in the aurora. Guess what tiny organism could be lighting up a beach. Predict when Noctilucent clouds will appear on the horizon. The more you talk about it, the more your ride transforms into a science lesson that looks exactly like a family memory."]}]}]}4:0 0

LUKE MARSH

0 0 0 0 0 0 0 0 0 0 0 0 0 0 0 0 0 0 0 0 0 0 0 0 0 0 0 0 0 0 0 0 0
0 0 0 0 0 0 0 0 0 0 0 0 0 0 0 0 0 0 0 0 0 0 0 0 0 0 0 0 0 0 0 0 0
0 0 0 0 0 0 0 0 0 0 0 0 0 0 0 0 0 0 0 0 0 0 0 0 0 0 0 0 0 0 0 0 0
0 0 0 0 0 0 0 0 0 0 0 0 0 0 0 0 0 0 0 0 0 0 0 0 0 0 0 0 0 0 0 0 0
0 0 0 0 0 0 0 0 0 0 0 0 0 0 0 0 0 0 0 0 0 0 0 0 0 0 0 0 0 0 0 0 0
0 0 0 0 0 0 0 0 0 0 0 0 0 0 0 0 0 0 0 0 0 0 0 0 0 0 0 0 0 0 0 0 0
0 0 0 0 0 0 0 0 0 0 0 0 0 0 0 0 0 0 0 0 0 0 0 0 0 0 0 0 0 0 0 0 0
0 0 0 0 0 0 0 0 0 0 0 0 0 0 0 0 0 0 0 0 0 0 0 0 0 0 0 0 0 0 0 0 0
0 0 0 0 0 0 0 0 0 0 0 0 0 0 0 0 0 0 0 0 0 0 0 0 0 0 0 0 0 0 0 0 0
0 0 0 0 0 0 0 0 0 0 0 0 0 0 0 0 0 0 0 0

8

OCEAN ODDITIES (EVEN IF YOU'RE LANDLOCKED)

Alien Sea Dwellers

If you could slip beneath the waves and swim into the blackout depths, you'd meet life that seems designed by beings from another world. The ocean is a vast dark lab where evolution has tried every wild idea imaginable, and some of the best-looking results look almost alien to us humans who nestle at the shore. In this quiet, inky world, creatures don't rely on color to attract mates or warn predators the way land animals do. They rely on light, pressure, and senses that humans barely understand.

Take the goblin shark, a creature that looks like it swam straight out of a science-fiction storyboard. Its snout is a long, flexible probe lined with sensors that can detect even a wisp of electricity from prey hiding in the dark. When the goblin shark bites, its jaw can shoot forward on a hinge—the kind of rapid strike that makes you imagine it has built-in retractable weaponry. It doesn't, of course, but the way it eats is a brilliant hack of nature's toolkit, shaped by a world with no sun and no easy snack bar.

Then there's the frilled shark, a living fossil that seems to have rolled off a prehistoric bookshelf. Its eel-like body coils and twists through the water with a submarine's quiet grace. Its seven pairs of frilly gills ripple like a delicate scarf as it glides along, hunting with slow, almost elegant patience. It's not flashy; it's patient, perfectly adapted to a life where food wears darkness like a cloak and meals arrive only when you're listening with your entire body.

Anglerfish are the bold stage performers of the midnight ocean. While most fish beach their approach under the sun's glare, the deepest dwellers glow from the inside out. A tiny lure dangles in front of a female's jaws, a light that attracts prey as surely as a neon sign attracts insects on a summer night. In these abyssal clubs, tiny male anglers take a different route altogether: they fuse with a female's body, sharing blood and survival in a world where even a bite can be life-threatening. It's not romance; it's a survival protocol that makes your high school chemistry periodic table look tame.

The viperfish, with its ribbon-like body and jaw-length fangs longer than most schoolyard pencils, lives in permanent twilight and above. Its photophores glow like stars along its flanks, and it uses a glowing lure to bait prey into striking range. Think of it as a predator that dresses for a midnight gala each night—glow, grab, gulp, and vanish back into the black.

Then there are the octopuses that wear their own kind of airbrushed attunement, like the dumbo octopus, whose ear-like fins flap as it glides. It seems to smile as it floats, a shy creature whose look of curiosity is enough to melt the fear of listeners in the car seat. The giant squid and the colossal squid, with eyes the size of dinner plates and tentacles that dive deep into the margins of rumor and myth, remind us that some ocean giants remain rare, secretive, and almost unfathomable enough to feel like legends living in a real sea.

Why do these creatures look so otherworldly? Because the deep ocean isn't just dark. It's persistently pressurized, cold, and silent enough to make any sound feel like a rumor. In such pressure, evolutionary experiments do not waste any part of the body that could help catch a bite. They develop light-producing organs called photophores so they can talk in a language the rest of us cannot hear—a glow that signals a friend, a lure for supper, or a warning in a language only a predator who knows bioluminescence can understand.

If you're listening aloud in the back seat, you'll notice the ocean's cast of characters feels like a parade from another planet. A single field guide could fill pages with pictures that look almost too strange to be real. But here's the kicker: every one of these strange appearances is a practical adaptation. The glow, the jaws, the flexible bodies, the slow stalks through the gloom—these are all tools designed to survive a domain where light is rare, space is huge, and dinner never clocks out. And what's more, some of these creatures keep changing even now, as scientists push deeper with better submersibles and brighter cameras.

The next time you pass a lighthouse or watch the sun glitter on the ocean's surface, imagine the hidden world that lies beneath—the world of aliens who never left Earth. You don't need a space suit to meet them. You just need to imagine a glow-in-the-dark fishing light that can attract a snack and a jaw that can snap on instinct. That's the magic of the deep sea: a place where normal rules bend until they're almost unrecognizable, and where the oddest neighbors you'll ever meet live beyond the light line.

Shipwrecked Puzzles

The sea is a graveyard for ships, but for backseat storytellers it's a treasure chest of puzzles waiting to be solved. When a vessel vanishes or a hull shows a strange sign of life after months at sea, the tale becomes less about the ship and more about the mystery—an invitation for curiosity to take the wheel and drive the conversation forward. In this section, we'll drift through a few famous shipwrecks and sea stories that are perfect for quick guesses, bold theories, and family debates.

One enduring mystery is the Mary Celeste, a merchant brigantine found adrift in the Atlantic in 1872 with no one aboard and a nearly full cargo. The ship's decks were clean, the sails in order, and the ship itself seemed seaworthy, yet six crew members and the captain were nowhere to be found. The lifeboat was missing but presumed not to have been used for an orderly evacuation. There were no signs of a fight, no obvious injuries, and no clue about what had become of the crew. The only sensible explanation seems to be something sudden and unforeseen: a weather shift, a chemical danger, or perhaps a decision to abandon ship that never happened because the crew never left their cabins. Or maybe the sea just kept its secrets and whispered them away to the deep.

Another haunting tale is the Ourang Medan, a ship name that rose from a horror story to a maritime legend. It is said that the crew sent out a distress call—then the message cut off in static and chaos and fire—and the ship eventually drifted into silence. When rescuers boarded, they found everyone dead, their faces twisted with fear and no obvious wounds. Supposedly the ship burned from the inside out, a mystery that invites every imaginable cause—from toxic cargo to unknown disease and even the work of a vengeful sea spirit. The truth is that there are many versions of this story, and none are confirmed with airtight certainty. Still, it's a classic in the backseat's mystery library because it asks a simple question: what do we do when we find a silent partner at sea?

Then there's the Joyita, a small cargo vessel found adrift in the South Pacific in 1955 with missing crew and passengers. The boat had crashed gear and some cargo still aboard, but the entire party seemed to have vanished without a trace or a cry for help. Its mystery rests not in a dramatic eruption but in a quiet, puzzling absence. No one can say whether it was a storm, a deliberate attempt to hide a crime, or a freak accident that left everyone to walk away from a life at sea. The Joyita doesn't scream answers; it invites you to debate the most likely explanation and to imagine what you would have done in such a moment.

What makes these stories so appealing on road trips is not just the drama but the open space they leave for guesses. You can spin a short theory: perhaps the crew found safer water and took a small boat; perhaps a sudden weather change forced everyone below deck at the same moment. You can also imagine the consequences: would your family have trusted the sea to deliver you, or would you have started drawing maps of escape routes and safe harbors as a game? The fun comes not from a single solution but from the conversation—the way a few details can morph into a dozen different endings.

CRAZY RANDOM FACTS FOR CAR RIDES

If you're looking for a quick game, try this: one person starts with a single clue from a shipwreck story, and each person in the car adds one new detail that could plausibly fit the tale. The goal isn't to prove a theory correct but to see how many ideas you can generate together before the next rest stop. You can switch ships every few minutes, or assign one person to be the "case file" keeper who folds in a fresh clue whenever the car hits a stretch of silence. The best part? Every family member can bring their own favorite era or locale to the conversation, from the arid Pacific to the foggy North Atlantic, and the backseat becomes a living maritime mystery club without a single subscription fee.

For older kids and grown-ups, you can expand the game into a quick investigative exercise. Write down a few known facts on an imaginary ship's logbook: cargo onboard, weather, voyage origin and destination, date, and a single unexplained clue. Then as you drive, everyone proposes a theory that connects the dots. The point isn't to land on one "correct" answer but to practice asking the right questions, spotting connections, and listening to each other's ideas. And if nothing else, you'll end a ride with a few more "What ifs" than you started with—the sign of a good trivia session that traveled well.

The ocean keeps its riddles close, but it loves a curious audience. That's you, the family stuffed into a car with a map, a window, and a couple of brave questions. Every shipwreck story is a doorway to imagination—an invitation to practice critical thinking in a light, social way, and a reminder that sometimes the best discoveries happen not at the destination but in the conversation you share along the way.

Salty Science

The ocean is not just a big blue blanket; it's a living experiment in fluids, temperatures, chemistry, and physics that happens on scales both enormous and minute. If you've ever wondered why the water in lakes and rivers behaves differently from seawater, you're about to get a shortcut course in why oceans work the way they do. The biggest clue is salinity, the proportion of dissolved salts in water. Seawater is salty because rocks on land wear away and rivers carry those salts to the sea. When water evaporates, it leaves salts behind, and when rivers keep delivering, the salinity stays in balance. The average salinity of the ocean is about 3.5 percent, or 35 grams of dissolved salts per liter of seawater. That might sound small, but it makes a huge difference in how water feels, how it conducts heat, and how it carries sound. It also affects how buoyant you feel when you swim; salty water makes you float a little higher than freshwater.

Salinity isn't perfectly constant, though. Some seas have lower salinity because of huge freshwater inputs from rivers or melting ice, and others have higher salinity where evaporation outpaces the supply. The surface of the ocean sits on a delicate balance sheet of heat and salt, a balance that drives the grand loop of the planet's climate—the thermohaline circulation. Here's the simple version that fits in the backseat: when water cools and gets salty enough, it sinks, and that sinking water drags warmer water from the surface along with it. This slow, global conveyor belt moves heat around the planet, helping to keep our coastal cities from freezing in winter and baking in summer. It's a reminder that even a ride with no Wi-Fi can carry a lesson about systems that are bigger than any single person.

Bioluminescence adds another spark to this salty science show. In the deepest parts of the ocean, many organisms produce their own light. The glow isn't just pretty; it's a practical tool for these creatures to lure prey, attract mates, or confuse predators. It's also a window into how light behaves in water. Seawater scatters light more than air, and it absorbs certain wavelengths faster than others. That's why deep-water scenes glow with blue-green hues that landlubbers rarely see up close. If you've ever wondered why a ship's wake glows at night, you've glimpsed a tiny shimmer of the same phenomenon—the light from tiny creatures or from electric-blue signaling that travels through water as the current shifts.

Sound in the ocean behaves in its own quirky way. Water transmits sound much faster and more efficiently than air. A whale song or a submarine ping can travel hundreds or thousands of miles with surprisingly little loss. That's also why sailors once learned to listen for distant thunder among waves during a storm, and why ships developed sonar to map the dark seafloor. If you drop a coin into a tub of seawater or splash a pan in the bath, you'll notice a little of that same underwater orchestra—tiny ripples that travel outward, only much, much bigger and deeper out at sea.

But the real star of salty science is water's density, which changes with both salinity and temperature. Cold, salty water sinks; warm, fresher water floats. This is the physics that makes sea ice float, and it's why the ocean has layers that don't mix as quickly as you might think. In the Arctic, for instance, sea ice forms and rejects salt into the surrounding water, creating cold, dense brine that sinks and helps drive the larger current systems. In sea life, density matters too: creatures adapt to life in layers where the water is lighter and warmer at the surface and heavy and dark below. It's a way of thinking that makes the world below the window a lot more interesting than a simple blue sheet.

Now, let's talk about waves. A wave is not a line of water moving forward along the surface, but a pattern of energy traveling through the water. The wind transfers energy to the water, creating a ripple that grows into a swell. The height and speed of waves depend on wind speed, how long the wind blows, and how long the fetch—the distance over which the wind has energy to act—gets. In the open ocean, you can have waves that travel hundreds of miles, preserving their rhythm until they finally crash on shore. It's a reminder that movement here isn't just motion; it's choreography.

Saltwater might also feel more buoyant because salt changes density. The more salt in the water, the more buoyant a body tends to be. This is why swimmers float more easily in the ocean than in freshwater lakes. And if you listen to the ocean right before a storm, you hear a different kind of conversation—the deeper water's sound is bolder, more intense, and ready to unleash power. The science behind all this is deceptively simple on the surface: heat, salt, and the way waves borrow energy from the wind. The deeper you go, the more complex the stories become, but for a road-trip audience, even one-liners make a big splash.

Now imagine explaining this to a kid who loves science and hates long lectures. You can invite them to think of the ocean as a giant, living experiment where the salt, the heat, and the sound all work together like a well-tuned band. You can point to the horizon and say, "That line of blue is the experiment's boundary. Beyond that is a world you can only learn about with a submarine camera and a brave scientist." Then you can pause and ask a simple question: why does the water at the beach feel colder than the water further out where it's deep? The answer is density and temperature; the deeper water is colder and denser, so it feels less friendly to a hand in the shallow splash. Quick, simple, and with a small aha that sticks.

That's salty science: a set of ideas about water that help explain why the oceans behave differently from the lakes and rivers we know from home. It's a toolkit for understanding the sea as a system, not a single mood ring. And it's the kind of knowledge that makes a late-night sky and a window seat conversation feel just a little more connected to the world beneath the surface.

Waves, Whirlpools, and Strange Currents

If the surface of the ocean is a stage, its underbelly is a playground for physics and geography. You can learn to read the sea by looking at the waves, currents, and the occasional whirligig of a whirlpool. This section is about how water moves, how it can surprise us with power, and how a car-ride chat can drift from curiosity to amazement in just a few sentences.

Waves begin with a whisper of wind and end as a chorus of energy traveling across vast distances. The water itself barely moves forward; instead, the wind's energy pushes on the surface, lifting and lowering waves in a dance that ripples for miles. The height of a wave depends on three simple ingredients: how strong the wind is, how long it blows, and how far the wind can push water in a straight line—the fetch. On the open sea, where there's no shore to interrupt the gust, waves can grow tall yet still travel quickly, with their crests standing like silver teeth across

CRAZY RANDOM FACTS FOR CAR RIDES

the horizon. When waves crash onto the shore, their energy is converted into foam, spray, and the spray's dramatic white line along the shoreline. The interesting twist is that people feel the power of a wave more when standing near the shore, where the water depth changes and the wave's energy funnels toward a single point of impact.

But not all motion is a traveling wave. You'll also hear people talk about rip currents—snapping fast flows that can pull a swimmer away from the beach. They aren't roaring like a river; they're narrow, focused pipes of water that squeeze through gaps between sandbars. If you're teaching kids about ocean safety, rip currents offer a clear lesson: do not fight the current; swim parallel to the shore until you're free of its grip. It's a simple rule, but it makes a real-world difference and turns a scary moment into a smart survival moment—perfect for backseat storytelling that doubles as a safety lesson.

Whirlpools are another dramatic reminder that big things can happen when water is forced into tight corners. They're not magical black holes—in most cases, they are powerful, winding currents driven by tides that swirl around islands or undersea seafloors. The Saltstraumen near Norway, for example, is one of the world's strongest tidal currents and can make the sea churn with glittering force that you could hear from far away. The whirlpool becomes a natural clock, ticking with the tides and reminding us that the planet is alive with motion even in what looks like still water. For the backseat, it's a vivid image: a clockwork river turning in a circle beneath the surface while the surface shows calm blue and ordinary waves.

In terms of big-picture currents, the Gulf Stream is the showstopper. This warm ocean current moves heat from the tropics northward along the eastern edge of the Americas and across the Atlantic. It is the sea's superhighway for warmth, a factor in climate patterns and a reason why some places around Europe feel milder than their latitude would suggest. We're talking about a current that shifts weather, freezes, and helps grow power plants of life somewhere else on the planet. It's not just a line on a map; it's a dynamic force that connects the weather outside your window to the world's far-off places. You can picture it as a conveyor belt of water that helps regulate temperatures while stirring life in ecosystems around the globe.

For those who like a little challenge, play a game of "What If?" during a rest stop. Pose a scenario: a strong wind from the sea's surface, a coastline shape, and a current that changes with the season. What kind of wave would you expect to see at the shore? What would happen to a leaf released into a particular current? The point is to encourage mental modeling: how do different pieces—wind, depth, coastline, and gravity—work together to shape what you see in the harbor and the open sea? It's a quick pop quiz you can do without tools, turning a simple drive into a small science classroom with a window for a blackboard.

And if you want to bring this back to story mode, imagine you're on a boat somewhere in the mixed-up zone where a tide meets a shallow reef. The water swirls and pulls in unexpected ways. A wave that looks ordinary from above suddenly carries a hidden grin—the sign of a current that's found a clever route around an obstacle. Your task is to trace cause and effect in your mind: why did the travel path change? How did the wind shift, and how did the water respond? These questions spark curiosity and deepen the sense that the ocean is more than a passive backdrop; it's a living map of how the world moves.

Ocean currents, waves, and whirlpools aren't just natural phenomena to memorize; they're stories you can read with your eyes. When you glance at the window, you're seeing more than water and sky; you're seeing the surface expression of currents and energy that have traveled thousands of miles from the planet's far corners. That realization makes every ride a little more magical, a little more connected to the planet we call home.

9

BUGS, SPIDERS, AND OTHER TINY SUPERVILLAINS

Amazing Insect Skills

Beneath the dashboard glare and the flutter of a passing insect in the car's air flow, insects are tiny engineers with mega skills. They wear hard shells as if armor, and they use physics like seasoned magicians. Consider the jumper of the insect world, the grasshopper and the flea, who can spring across gaps bigger than their own bodies. They don't just hop; they launch with a precision that would make a gymnast nod in respect. The sky is not off-limits to this crew. Dragonflies dart and hover with a steadiness that would impress a helicopter pilot, catching objects in midair with a snap of their jaws. And while you blink, ants are carrying crumbs several times their own body weight, building tiny roads and rafts in a single afternoon while you're stuck in traffic behind a stubborn SUV.

Insects also wear disguises like master illusionists. Leaf insects in leafy dresses look so much like real leaves that people walking past swear they saw a breeze instead of a body. Some beetles mimic the scent or shape of other bugs so predators get a whiff of nothing but confusion. Camouflage isn't merely pretty; it's protection in motion, a tactical advantage that lets a tiny creature survive in a world that seems designed for giants.

A lot of insect genius hides in a little mouthful of silk. Silkworms and other silk producers spin threads that humans have turned into clothes and bandages and even parachute cords. Silk is famously strong and light, tougher by weight than many materials, and it comes from creatures the size of your thumbnail. Insects also craft elaborate homes and cocoons, weaving a safe world around themselves and their eggs.

Defense is another special skill set. The bombardier beetle is basically a tiny firework artist, mixing chemicals inside its abdomen and blasting a hot, stinging spray when trouble comes close. It's not just about making trouble; it's about staying alive in a world full of hungry mouths. Some aphids and scale insects live in what looks like a calm city of leaves, yet they can recruit worker insects to shield them from danger with synchronized defense moves.

But the most astonishing superpower might be teamwork. Ants and termites are not just "groups of bugs"—they are complex societies. They farm fungus, herd aphids for honeydew, and coordinate elaborate tunnel maps in the soil. Their communication smells like a secret recipe, a blend of pheromones that tells a whole colony what to do next, exactly where to go, and when to stand down. Insects show that even a creature tiny enough to fit on your fingertip can run a city. The natural world is full of such micro-metropolises, and the car's window can serve as a miniature tour of their astonishing engineering and teamwork.

Speed, stealth, and survival have become second nature for many insects. They are not merely pests sneaking into a picnic; they are survivors who turn the earth's smallest pieces into a grand, buzzing orchestra of life. Every wingbeat is a reminder that size is not a limit, and that even the most unassuming creature can wield a surprising superpower.

Spider Myths vs Facts

Spiders pop up in every kid's fear and every parent's 'are you sure that's safe?' moment. Yet the more you know about them, the less they resemble the big, scary boogeymen of bedtime stories. Here's how to separate truth from tall tales, with a few giggles along the way.

Myth: Spiders are out to bite us at the first chance they get. Fact: Most spiders would rather escape a room than bite a person. They're shy, not aggressive, and they fear creatures larger than they are, which includes most humans. A spider's bite is usually a last resort—like a tiny alarm signal—only in self-defense when it feels cornered. In a car full of people, a spider will probably disappear behind the glove compartment before anyone even notices it.

Myth: All spiders have eight eyes and perfect night vision. Fact: Spiders do carry eight eyes, but vision is a mixed bag depending on the species. Some have excellent daytime eyesight, others rely on sensing vibrations through their webs or the ground. A few see so little that they might as well be wearing blindfolds, yet they navigate their world with silken traps, tactile hairs, and super-sensitive nerves. The moral: eyes are not everything in a spider's toolbox.

Myth: Spiders spin webs to catch every meal they eat. Fact: Not all spiders weave webs, and many don't catch every bite from a web anyway. Some spiders hunt on the ground; others chase prey with lightning-fast bursts of speed. Webs are not advertisements for every meal but rather efficient catch networks for certain lucky evenings. Some spiders live indoors and barely use their silk at all, choosing stealth and surprise instead of a sticky trap.

Myth: Black widows and brown recluses are everywhere and deadly. Fact: Venomous does not mean aggressive. A bite from these spiders is rare, and modern medicine makes the odds of a serious consequence much smaller than they used to be. Most encounters end with the spider simply retreating. If you do see a spider that makes you uneasy, it's perfectly fine to coax it outside with a jar and a sheet—safely, of course—so everyone can breathe easier.

Myth: Spiders can burrow and live under your skin. Fact: That's a movie plot, not biology. Spiders inhabit real places like corners of walls, the undersides of leaves, and the nooks between books. They can make homes in a garden shed or in the gaps of your glove box, but they stay above the skin and prefer the freedom of the great outdoors whenever possible.

Spiders are experts at using what they have: silk that can weave a city-wide web or a tiny curtain to cover an egg sac, fangs that deliver venom with surgical calm, and legs that sense the world through vibrations and chemical cues. They aren't villains by default; many are masters of quiet, careful survival. The more we learn, the more we realize that myths about eight-legged monsters often hide a curious, clever, and surprisingly helpful creature that just wants a little space and a chance to do its job.

The World's Weirdest Worms

Worms aren't glamorous in the way dragons are, but they can be incredibly fascinating in their own squiggly, wiggly ways. This is a tour of some of the world's most curious worm relatives—creatures that keep soil healthy, bodies flexible, and science buzzed with curiosity.

Earthworms are the soil's best friends. They tunnel through dirt, turning dead leaves and minerals into fertile soil that helps plants drink up nutrients. They breathe through their skin, which means they need a constant moister environment to stay happy and healthy. Their bodies are segmented, like a tiny engine with many moving parts, and they can regrow little pieces if they get sliced, which is a perfect reminder that even gentle creatures can be surprisingly resilient. Earthworms remind us that the ground beneath our wheels is not empty; it's a living, breathing network that supports every garden, field, and roadside flower bed.

Ribbon worms and flatworms trip the light fantastic in a different way. The ribbon worms shoot out a long, gliding proboscis to capture prey, sometimes wrapping it with a cunning stretch that seems almost magical. Flatworms, including planarians, can regenerate lost body parts in ways that would make a science fiction writer jealous. If you've ever heard that a small creature can become two, you're half-right—their regenerative talents can be spectacularly prodigious, though not always simple and predictable. Planarians particularly teach us about stretching boundaries, literally and scientifically.

Nematodes might be the most mysterious of all. These microscopic worms are everywhere—so common you could unearth millions in a single handful of soil. Some nematodes help farmers by feasting on pests, while others are parasites that require caution in medical contexts. It's a reminder that small doesn't mean simple; some tiny creatures act as invisible gardeners for ecosystems, balancing populations and keeping nature's ledger in check. They are the quiet workers behind the scenes, often slipping past the human eye yet playing a pivotal role in the health of soils, crops, and natural habitats.

Then there are the bigger, bolder cousins in the worm family—the sword-like gar are sometimes called bobbit worms for their fearsome jaws, the sea's ancient ambush artists that lie buried in the sand waiting for a prey's shadow. Their energy speaks to a world where predators evolve extraordinary tools for survival, even in the ocean's most dimly lit corners. Casting the spotlight outside the sea, the hammerhead worms with their T-shaped heads throw another curveball into the worm world. Some of these flatworms can glide through moist soil, breaking into sections to generate new life, a reminder that the line between life, division, and growth can be wonderfully blurry in nature.

Important to remember is that many worms are not just creepy-crawly performers; they are ecological engineers. Fireflies may steal most of the nightly glow, but glow-in-the-dark worms—where they occur—show how light and life can be a shared stage. Fireflies aren't worms, but their cousins remind us that light can be a serious party trick in the animal kingdom. The bottom line: worms come in many shapes, sizes, and talents, and they're some of the planet's best teachers about patience, resilience, and the quiet power of underground labor.

Tiny Heroes, Too

If you've ever thought that small things can't make a big difference, this section is your reminder that minuscule creatures can be major helpers to ecosystems and even to us. Tiny creatures do not merely exist to squeal out a quick scare in a car ride; they actively shape the world in ways that touch our daily lives.

Pollinators are the star performers here. Bees buzz from flower to flower, spreading pollen that helps plants reproduce. Without these tiny workers, many fruits, vegetables, and crops wouldn't grow as abundantly as they do. Butterflies, moths, and even some beetles join the party, painting a picture of a thriving ecosystem where plants and animals collaborate in a timeless dance. The lesson is simple: small visitors can have a huge impact on what ends up on our plates and in the stores we visit on road trips.

Soil dwellers, like earthworms and many tiny arthropods, perform a quieter magic. They loosen soil, mix nutrients, and create air pockets that roots need. This aeration helps plants drink more easily and keeps gardens alive, proving that the world beneath our tires is busy at work while we're busy moving forward.

Then there are creatures whose job is pest control, a natural army of helpers that minimize the need for pesticides. Nematodes and certain wasps hunt pest insects, acting as tiny guardians of crops. Bumblebees and other pollinators aren't the only workers here; parasitoid wasps quietly keep pest populations in check, balancing the ecosystem's numbers with a gentle touch.

Tiny heroes also appear in surprising places, like the bacteria and fungi inside our bodies and in the soil. Microbes help break down food, recycle nutrients, and even shield plants from disease. In a car full of kids, a short fact can become a long conversation about how life exists in layers—how big things interact with the tiny, and how the most powerful processes often happen out of sight.

Like all good road trips, the right mix of tiny heroes can turn a ride into a journey with science in the passenger seat. Tiny creatures teach us to look closer, ask more questions, and see the world as a place where even the smallest participant can change the game. In the grand scheme of things, miniature life is not just a feature of a science classroom; it is a living, breathing chorus that keeps the Earth humming along as we travel.

10

SPORTS, GAMES, AND PLAYGROUND TRIVIA

Strange Rules You Won't Believe

Sport is full of rules, and some of them read like they were written by a referee who loves puzzles. When you hear about them, you instantly picture a backseat full of giggles as you try to explain them aloud between sips of juice and the hum of the tires. These are the kinds of rules that make you tilt your head and say, wait, that's legal? The first one is a classic that sounds more like a comedy sketch than a rule book: the infield fly rule in baseball. Picture this: with runners on base and less than two outs, a pop-up that would be an easy catch to retire the batter somehow results in the batter being out automatically. The defensive team can't use a trick to double up runners the normal way, because the rule makes it so the fielder can't take advantage of a pop-up to cause chaos on the basepaths. It's designed to keep the play fair and a little bit magical, and it has the same effect as a gentle reminder from a patient umpire: we're playing a game, so let's keep it honest and fun. For kids hearing this for the first time, it's a moment that feels like discovering a hidden hatch in a video game, where a complex piece of knowledge unlocks a new way to think about play.

Then there's soccer and the offside rule, which can feel almost like a plot twist written by someone who loves suspense. The moment the ball is passed, if your teammate is ahead of the ball and nearer to the opponent's goal than the second-to-last defender, you're in an offside position. That means you can't touch the ball until it's gone back behind you, back onside. It sounds simple, but in fast games the rule looks like a little race against time and geometry. It's not cruel or confusing once you see the logic: you want the attacking team to earn their goal by skill and timing, not just by standing still and waiting for a perfect moment to sprint. For kids, the best way to picture it is to imagine a line drawn by an invisible referee from the ball to the goal. If you cross that line too early, you're playing yourself out of the action, and the moment passes you by.

Cricket adds another flavor of oddball logic with the no-ball and the free hit. If the bowler oversteps the crease or bowls illegally, the next delivery is a free hit, and the batter can swing away with fewer consequences for a mistake. It's a rule that makes the scoring more dramatic, like a video game power-up that shifts the odds in the player's favor—until the next over, when normal rules return. It's the kind of thing that makes fans grin and kids whisper, "That's not fair... or is it?" because the game rewards precision and a little bit of luck in the same breath.

Tennis has a few quirks that feel almost theatrical on a sunny afternoon. The let on a serve is a famous one: if the ball hits the net but still lands in the service box, you get a redo. That's not a loss; it's a polite nudge from the universe to try again if the net was just in a mood that day. It's a moment that invites patience and a touch of humor —perfect for a car ride when the odds of a perfect serve are slim. And in children's versions of sports, even the things that seem small can become jokes you tell at the back of the car: the time a ball hits the net and the server sighs, "Let's try that again."

If you've ever wondered how games like extra-time end, you'll find the concept of sudden death or "golden goal" entertaining and a little dramatic. In some contexts, the first team to score in extra time claims victory. It's a sprint to the finish that turns a long game into a movie trailer moment—short, intense, and easy to replay in your head as you drive from one destination to the next. The mercy rule also loves a good punchline, especially in youth sports. When a game becomes one-sided late in the proceedings, this rule steps in to keep things friendly and fun, ending the match early to protect the players' enthusiasm and avoid a meltdown in the backseat.

These five or six examples aren't just about rules; they're about the character of a game. They show how athletes and fans alike adapt to the quirks of the sport, turning potential confusion into shared laughter and curiosity. The result is a kind of mental warm-up for the road: every rule is a tiny puzzle, and every solved puzzle is a new joke to tell at the next stoplight. The surprise isn't that sports have strange rules; it's that those rules can spark quick debates, goofy what-if questions, and playful demonstrations that bring everyone into the game—no Wi-Fi required.

In this section, you'll hear about a few more odd, real-world rules with a light-hearted twist. We'll pair each rule with a quick story or a quick "would you rather?" moment that fits naturally into a car ride. These aren't exhaustive manuals; they're spark-plug ideas you can pull out on a long drive when you want to spark a little healthy competition without getting bogged down in the technicalities. So the next time a pop-fly lands in the glove of an umpire, or the ball sails past a defender in a split second, you'll have a ready-made way to turn that moment into a memory—one that leaves everyone smiling and curious about how the next rule will change the game.

Wild World Records

If you've ever watched sports galore on TV and thought, I bet someone could do that for real, you're not alone. The world is full of records that read like dares and sound like they were born in a dare-devil's dream. Some are astonishing feats of strength or speed, others celebrate teamwork, rhythm, or endurance, and a good chunk of them come with numbers so big they feel like a carnival trick. All of them are real enough to, at the very least, make you say, "No way!" at the top of your lungs. And because this is a car ride book designed for quick smiles, we'll keep the facts vivid, the numbers true where they're known, and the explanations kid-friendly.

Let's start with the ones that feel almost mythical in their simplicity. The fastest 100 meters ever run by a human is a record you've probably heard of: Usain Bolt clocked 9.58 seconds in 2009. Listen to that number and imagine the speed. That is faster than a lot of everyday tasks in a single breath, and it makes you think about how your own feet work when you sprint after a dog in the park or race to catch a ball at recess. It's a reminder that human bodies can push their limits to levels that look superhuman from a car seat window.

Or consider Wilt Chamberlain's legendary 100-point game in 1961. Picture a player scoring a hundred points in one game—a number that seems almost fictional, like something you'd see on a scoreboard in a sci-fi movie.

The sheer endurance and focus required to reach that many points makes kids whisper, wow, that's not just skill; that's a whole lot of practice, discipline, and a taste for big challenges. It's a reminder that records are not about being the best at a single thing forever; they're about showing what's possible when someone dedicates themselves to a goal.

Another headline in the world of records comes from endurance and strategy: Michael Phelps won a total of 23 Olympic gold medals across five games. That is a treasure chest of victories—more golds than most people will ever see in a lifetime. It doesn't just celebrate speed or strength; it celebrates consistency, mental preparation, and the ability to stay focused across years of training and competition. When you're strapped into a long car ride, that kind of perseverance can feel like a roadmap to staying committed to any goal, whether it's finishing a long trip or mastering a tricky new trick on the basketball court in your driveway.

In the realm of ball control and power, there are also jaw-dropping moments like the sport's fastest recorded tennis serve. A pitcher of pace—an ace that rockets past the opponent's racket—shows how precision and physics can combine to create a moment that feels almost like magic. The ball leaves the racquet, seemingly in slow motion, then whoosh, it's in the service box before anyone can blink. This serves as a quick lesson: tiny adjustments—

angle, speed, height—can make a huge difference in performance.

We can't ignore Kipchoge's marathon moment, either. In a landmark event designed to test human limits, he completed a marathon in under two hours, a target many people joked about as impossible—yet it wasn't officially recognized as a world record in the traditional sense due to the conditions and setup. It remains a bold statement about human potential. And in the same vein, Kipchoge's official record time in a standard competitive marathon—two hours, one minute, thirty-nine seconds in Berlin—still frames an astonishing achievement. It's a reminder that the line between what's technically a record and what captures our imagination can blur when a person dares to push the edge of possibility.

To round out the playlist of "wild" records, consider the long-ball legends: the longest official drive in golf charts a moment when skill meets a favorable wind, give or take, producing a distance that becomes a story of its own. The idea of a drive that travels hundreds of yards feels like a dare you might issue to a friend in a backseat game of "who can hit the garage door from the curb." And in the world of ball accuracy and power, the fastest ever recorded tennis ball speed and the most dominant performance in a single Olympics are proof that sports aren't just about winning; they're about finding a moment where human ability and possibility align in a way that makes the rest of us feel a little taller.

If you've ever wondered what makes a record feel so exciting, here's the throughline: records aren't just about numbers, they're about stories—stories of stubborn practice, strange luck, and the moment when a person says, "I'm going to try something that seems impossible." For kids, those stories grow into a belief that goals can be bigger than the car's windshield, that curiosity can be a kind of fuel, and that with a plan and a dash of courage, you can turn a rumor of a dare into a real achievement.

In this chapter we've looked at human speed, monumental endurance, and mind-bending consistency. We've learned that the world of records is as diverse as a road trip playlist: there are songs about velocity, endurance, precision, and teamwork, all inspiring the same feeling—wow, that was cool, and I bet I could do something worth talking about on the next leg of the journey.

The Science of Winning

Winning isn't only about talent; it's also about tiny, practical science you can feel with your senses as you ride along. Speed, balance, reaction time, and strategy all have science behind them, but you don't need a lab bench to understand them. You can see the ideas in action with a few simple observations and mental games that fit neatly into a family car ride. The first big idea is momentum—the idea that moving bodies want to stay moving and that getting them going quickly can help you stay ahead once you're on a roll. When you run toward a ball or a friend throws you a soft pass, your body's momentum is the engine that carries you forward. The trick, and the fun, is to channel that momentum smoothly, not with wild flailing but with controlled, precise movements that come from practice and awareness.

Balance is another key ingredient. On a bicycle, on skates, or even on a tightrope line in a playground, balance is all about keeping your center of gravity over your base of support. A slight lean in the wrong direction, and your body will correct itself—usually with a quick wobble, followed by a safe landing. In sports, this translates to better posture, stronger hold on a ball, and more reliable footwork. The body learns balance with practice, but the brain learns it even faster with good feedback: small, quick adjustments in knee bend, hip tilt, and shoulder alignment can make a dramatic difference in performance.

Reaction time—the speed of your brain turning an observation into a decision and your body into action—is a playful challenge in road trips. You can test it with simple games that require you to clap when you hear a sound or to catch a small object before it hits the floor. The better your brain and body communicate, the quicker you respond. Anthropologists and scientists describe reaction time as a skill that can be trained with quick, controlled practice. And the best part is that you can do it anywhere: a kitchen, a classroom, or a backseat, as long as you're paying attention and keeping it light.

There's a neat bridge between science and sport: aerodynamics and grip, the invisible forces that help you move faster and with more control. In car seats, these ideas come alive in how we position our bodies while playing a quick game of pretend to be a top sprinter, or how we adjust the way we hold a toy ball or a snack bag to reduce air resistance. Sneakers with a grippy sole, smooth floor underfoot, and well-timed steps all work together to maximize traction and efficiency. Teachers and parents can use these ideas at home or at a park to show kids how to move with less effort yet more power—like a secret trick that makes every step feel a little lighter and a little more precise.

The psychology of winning is the quiet partner to the physical side. Confidence, focus, and a positive mindset don't require a lab; they come from small rituals and positive reinforcement. You can teach kids to visualize a successful finish, to break a big challenge into small, doable steps, and to treat mistakes as opportunities to learn rather than as personal failures. The brain responds to this kind of approach with calm and a readiness to try again, which makes the next attempt a little less scary and a little more fun. That combination of mental training and physical practice is the heart of why players get better over time: it's not just talent; it's preparation and perseverance.

If you want to see the science at work, try a few quick, kid-friendly experiments during a ride. Measure reaction times by tapping at a signal and counting the moment your friend taps you back. Balance can be explored by carefully walking a straight line with your eyes closed and then opening them to check your wobble. Quick bursts of speed can be compared with and without gloves or with different kinds of shoes, to feel how grip and friction matter. The more you play with these ideas, the more you notice in everyday life—the way cars grip the road, the way street signs reflect the wind, and the way your own body naturally adapts to moving through space.

The science of winning is not about turning someone into a super-athlete overnight; it's about recognizing that your body and your brain are a team, and that small, consistent improvements compound over time. On long trips or quick errands alike, you can turn any moment into a mini-training session—light, fun, and entirely doable without leaving the seat. The next time you watch a game and notice a perfect change of pace or an almost perfect pass, you'll know you're seeing the science of winning in real time, and you'll have a ready-made conversation starter to share with your travel companions.

In summary, the physics and psychology of sport operate in plain sight: momentum, balance, reaction time, grip, and mindset come together to shape how fast you move, how steadily you control a ball, and how calmly you respond when the pressure builds. When you understand these ideas, you can turn a simple car ride into a classroom on wheels—one that doesn't feel like school at all, but like a game where every observation nudges you toward a better move, a sharper thought, and a bigger smile.

Car-Ride Challenges

Challenge ideas that fit a car ride are the secret sauce of this chapter. They turn steady miles into a string of goofy competitions, quick debates, and surprising discoveries. The best part is that these activities require almost nothing: just curiosity, a little courage to speak up, and a willingness to laugh together. You can weave a few of these into a single trip or stretch them across a week of rides, stopping only when the wheels stop rolling. The rules are simple and flexible, designed to keep every passenger engaged without turning the car into a chaotic arena. If you want to up the stakes, you can add simple point systems, but the true payoff is the shared memory and the burst of laughter that travels with you long after you've parked.

First, a quick-fire round that keeps knowledge fresh and conversation lively. You narrate a short fact about a sport or a famous record, and everyone has to decide whether it's true or false by shouting out their guess. If someone guesses correctly, they earn a point; if they're wrong, they owe the car a giggle as a penalty. The trick is to pick a mix of easy and tricky facts—things that a 10-year-old could recognize and a curious teen might question. You can also turn this into a rapid "fact or fib" round by telling two facts and one made-up rumor about a sport that week and letting the crew spot the fake.

Another favorite is the "choose-your-own-adventure" trivia chase. The driver reads a prompt like, "Name three world records that sound like dares," and the passengers take turns adding entries, with the driver deciding which answer counts based on a simple rule: it must be verifiable, reasonable, and child-friendly. The more outrageous the examples, the better the laughs, as long as the conversation stays clean and kind. This game is perfect for backseat debates and for teaching kids how to back up a claim with a simple explanation—"Why do you think that's true?" becomes a fun, not-serious question that invites everyone to participate.

For players who love a quick physical challenge, you can invent tiny, seat-friendly movements that test balance and coordination without requiring space. One example is a "finger tennis" challenge where players use only their fingertips to tap the index finger of another person, counting the successful taps in a 20-second window. It's silly, it builds hand-eye coordination, and it requires almost no room. You can scale it up by assigning a trick shot in your own version of a car-based sport—like balancing a small soft ball on the back of your hand while another person gently taps it to keep it aloft. The key is to keep it light and safe, turning each attempt into a small triumph and a family story to tell when you reach your destination.

If your crew enjoys a little strategy with their trivia, try a "Would You Try It?" game. Propose wacky hypothetical questions that mix sports and everyday life—things like, would you rather be an incredible long-distance swimmer who never forgets a stroke or a marathon runner with the world's most powerful sprint but always finishes second? The point isn't whether the choice is fair; the point is to listen, debate kindly, and practice a bit of empathy as you consider someone else's perspective. You'll be surprised how much perspective and humor you gain just by hearing people's explanations.

Finally, don't forget to celebrate the small wins. The moment someone answers a question correctly or comes up with a clever explanation is a moment to praise. A simple "nice job explaining that" or "great memory on that fact" goes a long way toward keeping the ride friendly, energetic, and inclusive. The goal is not to crush the game with points but to fill the car with laughter, curiosity, and a sense that learning something new together is as rewarding as reaching the next stop.

With these four sections, you can turn any journey into a rolling classroom of fun, where facts mingle with jokes, challenges evolve into stories, and curiosity stays lit from city to city. The sports world becomes a playground of ideas you can explore aloud, and the drive itself becomes a shared adventure rather than a mere mile marker. Keep the questions coming, lean into the laughter, and watch how quickly a car ride becomes your family's favorite classroom on wheels.

11

LANGUAGE, WORDS, AND SILLY SAYINGS

Words That Sound Fake (But Aren't)

Words have a habit of fooling our ears. Some of the oddest-looking terms in English sound like they belong in a cartoon, yet they're perfectly real and useful in everyday chatter. This section is a playful tour of real words that sound fake, thrilling in their silliness, and surprisingly practical once you know what they mean. Start by reading them aloud. You will hear the dance of consonants and vowels that gives language its zing, the moment when a word feels almost like a joke you already know but didn't quite expect to be real.

Kerfuffle. It sounds made up, but kerfuffle means a fuss or commotion. It's one of those words that shows how quickly our mouths can pivot from normal to exuberant when a tiny sputter of sound appears in the air. Its origin trickles in from Scottish roots, and the way it rolls off the tongue makes it the perfect word to throw into a story about a family parking lot scandal or a pet's dramatic escape from the kitchen. You can use it to describe a minor scandal or a big mix-up, and suddenly everyone in the car is smiling at the exaggeration.

Flummox. If you have ever been stumped and felt wildly perplexed, you know flummox in your bones. The word carries a weight of bafflement that is both comic and endearing. Its origin is a little murky, but that mystery only adds to its charm. When a kid can't remember the spelling of a word or a grown-up can't locate the car keys, a well-timed flummox becomes the setup for a quick joke and a shared groan.

Gobbledygook. This one is a masterclass in sound. Gobbledygook describes language that is filled with jargon and nonsense, especially in bureaucratic contexts. It sounds exactly how long explanations can feel when you are tired or trying to tune out. The word itself seems to wobble and flap its own vowels, mirroring the chaos it describes. It's perfect for pointing at a confusing instruction manual or a far too fancy sign in a shopping mall and turning it into a family joke.

Poppycock and nincompoop. These two bring a bounce to the backseat. Poppycock is a historical term for nonsense, while nincompoop refers to a silly or foolish person. Both are light, friendly, and safe for kids. Poppycock's old-timey flavor makes it a delightful reminder that language ages like a good cheese—getting funkier with time. Nincompoop is the kind of word a parent can slip into conversation to get a smile or a giggle from even the most stubborn rider.

Widdershins. This is a fancy word for moving counterclockwise, or simply going in the wrong direction relative to the usual flow. It sounds like a spell from a fantasy novel, and in a car with a child who loves stories, it becomes a cue for a little imaginative game: pretend you are navigating a magical clock where everything moves a tad widdershins. The pronunciation itself is a mini lesson in rhythm, and the meaning invites a tiny ecology of directional thinking that fits well into map-reading inside a car.

Bumbershoot and snollygoster. Bumbershoot is a cheerful umbrella, a perfect hello to a rainy-day mood in the backseat. It pairs beautifully with snollygoster, a word for a clever, perhaps untrustworthy person, a bit of a mouthful that always draws a nod and a curious question. Both words carry theatrical weight, inviting kids to engage with the idea that language loves drama as much as it loves information.

From these few examples you can see a pattern. Real words can sound like fiction, yet they carry precise meanings and histories. The trick is to read them aloud, to hear how their sounds cue the mood of a sentence.

When a kid learns kerfuffle and follows it with gobbledygook in a story about a school project, the room fills with laughter and a sense of discovery. The vocabulary becomes a game, not a quiz, and the car ride becomes a rolling classroom where curiosity is always invited and never forced.

The key takeaway is texture. Real words carry texture, personality, and a hint of origin. They can be playful, pompous, or plain practical, and they all have a story to tell. Try saying a couple of these words with different emphases, as if you are performing an impromptu mini-sketch on the side of the road. You will notice the way emphasis can change a joke from a stumble to a showstopper. In a family car, that transformation is priceless. It turns a routine ride into a memory with a signal flare of laughter and a prompt for conversation that can continue long after the miles pass by.

Where Phrases Came From

Phrases are little time machines. They carry echoes of the people, places, and problems that gave birth to them, and when you drop one into a conversation, you're inviting a tiny history lesson without a textbook in sight. The origin stories behind everyday sayings can be either delightfully mundane or strikingly odd, but they always offer a spark for discussion and a moment to imagine the past turning a wheel inside the present.

Let the ice break in your car, and you're leaning into break the ice. This phrase comes from ships in frozen ports. When the cold blocked a ship's normal course, sailors literally broke the ice to make room for boats to pass and trade to resume. The imagery has stayed even when the world moved from rope and sail to engines and GPS. The same feeling of starting something before you are ready, but with a little more friendliness, makes the phrase a natural go-to for first conversations on a trip or a new activity with friends and family. It is a reminder that beginnings don't have to be formal, and a warm word can thaw a tense moment in an instant.

Spill the beans, a phrase you have probably heard in markets and meetings, likely began as a vote tally system in ancient Greece. Beans were used to cast ballots; spilling the beans would reveal the outcome. The modern usage has drifted far from its original purpose, but the image remains clear and vivid. It's a perfect kickoff for a story about secret plans or big surprises in the backseat, a reminder that some truths are better told in a moment of laughter than with a stern face.

Let the cat out of the bag seems darker than it sounds, but the history is playful. In medieval markets, traders sometimes sold piglets in bags. If a cat slipped out instead, the deception was exposed. The phrase has traveled well beyond its literal heart, now meaning to reveal a secret unexpectedly. This one invites kids to guess which secrets are safe to tell and which should stay hidden for a brighter surprise later in the trip, turning a simple reveal into a moment of shared astonishment or a silly misunderstanding.

Kick the bucket carries a different flavor. It comes from a time when slaughtering animals or hanging ropes required a setting that involved a bucket near the animal's feet. The bucket could become kicked during the process, and the grim origin softened into a more general meaning: to die. In a kid-friendly retelling, you can frame it as a rough history that helps explain why we keep our language curious and flexible, even if the topic itself is solemn. The lesson is that phrases can travel far from their starting point and still be useful in everyday speech.

Break out the whole nine yards, meanwhile, sports a mystery of its own. There are many theories about where this phrase came from, including stories about military gun belts and fabric bolt lengths. The truth matters less than the feeling: a phrase that signals going all in, giving your best effort, and leaving nothing on the table. It's a perfect prompt for a game in the backseat: who can tell the most complete version of a story or complete a task with all nine yards of effort? The ambiguity invites curiosity, debate, and more giggles as everyone hammers out their own versions of the origin.

Raining cats and dogs, an expression that paints a cartoon sky, likely emerged in the 17th century, when heavy rain could literally sweep through streets like a flood of unlikely creatures. The exact origin is debated, but the image sticks. Use it to describe a downpour during a road trip, turning weather into a vivid moment for picture-book storytelling.

Rounding out the set, you have a handful of practical phrases that feel like games you can play with your own family lore: why does this phrase exist, what image does it conjure, and what new version can you invent for your next car ride? The answers are always in the listening—the same way a road trip reveals new corners of familiar places.

The history behind phrases is not just trivia; it is a way to invite conversation about culture, work, and life in different eras. When you share these origins, you give children a sense that language grows with people, from farmers and sailors to teachers and storytellers. That idea feels especially satisfying on long drives, when stories can stretch as the road does. So keep a few favorites ready, and when a phrase lands in a conversation, pause, tell its origin, and watch the eyes light up as curiosity takes the wheel for a moment.

You can mix and match origins with the mood of the ride. A silly misheard phrase might become a nickname for the family, while a history-rich origin becomes a quick mini-lesson and a chuckle. Either way, these origin stories connect language to life, inviting everyone in the car to participate in the journey—not just observe it from the backseat window.

Tongue Twisters and Tricky Sounds

Tongue twisters are the snackable, giggle-inducing snacks of language. They are short, sharp challenges that wake up the mouth and loosen up the jaw. The best part is that they are perfectly safe for kids and endlessly entertaining for adults. The trick is not to punish a stumble but to celebrate a successful delivery. The room, or the car, becomes a tiny stage where the narrator tries to shove as many tricky sounds as possible into a single, rapid sentence. The more you laugh, the looser your tongue becomes, and the more confident you and your crew grow in their ability to say almost anything clearly, even when the road is bumpy.

She sells seashells by the seashore is a classic for a reason. Its soft sibilants—those s sounds—make the mouth push and pull in a rapid dance. Peter Piper picked a peck of pickled peppers is a parade of plosive p sounds that feel like a tiny workout for the lips, especially when spoken with speed. Unique New York keeps the vowels honest, with a tight grip on the tricky U and E vowels that easily blend into a muddle if you rush. Red lorry, yellow lorry plays with the consonant cluster between l and r, a challenge that leaves even grownups grinning at their own silliness.

Then there are the more modern and casual favorites. One quick challenge is to say Irish wristwatch three times fast. It combines both a tricky name and a tricky combination of r and w sounds. The trick here is to start slowly and build speed while keeping clarity. A few rounds of the classic toy boat and toy boat twist will leave the car with smoke-free lungs and a chorus of laughter as you catch the shape of the words you are trying to sculpt.

Practical tips for quick-friendly practice lay the groundwork for long-term play. Start by saying the tongue twister slowly, then gradually increase speed while maintaining accuracy. Pause when a racer in the car trips over a word, then laugh, reset, and try again. The important part is the shared energy: everyone tries, nobody gets punished for stumbles, and the energy of the game lifts the mood for the whole ride. If you want to turn a twist into a game, challenge your fellow travelers to produce the clearest, most dramatic rendition, or record a quick family reel with a phone to preserve the moment for later laughter.

These challenges have two practical benefits beyond the giggles. First, they improve pronunciation and speech confidence, especially for younger travelers who are learning how their mouths make sound. Second, they create a shared moment of vulnerability and humor that makes the trip feel shorter and much more memorable. The simplest twister—say it once, say it again, then make it a game to see who can improve the most by the time the next rest stop arrives—can be a surprising engine of family bonding, education, and pure backseat joy.

Secret Codes and Slang

Language loves disguises. Secret codes and slang are language with a wink. They let groups create inside jokes, punish boredom with cleverness, and surprise strangers with a tone that says we belong here, right now. This section looks at how words become coded messages and how slang travels across ages and into the car's conversation, where a simple phrase can carry a world of meaning in two syllables.

A classic example is Pig Latin, a playful language game that hides a meaning just enough to be amusing. To translate into Pig Latin, you move the first consonant sounds to the end of the word and add ay. For example, apple becomes appleay, and school becomes oolschay. The result is a cipher that kids love to play with on long trips, turning ordinary sentences into a playful code that feels like a secret club's language. The rules are simple, but the possibilities are endless, and the kids quickly learn to listen for the rhythm and the trick of the conversion.

Another enduring favorite is leet speak, a playful alteration of letters that makes simple words look mischievous. Replacing E with 3, A with 4, or I with 1 creates a digital wink to the reader. It looks like a puzzle and acts like a password that invites curiosity. The most exciting part is watching kids discover their own substitutions, turning a dull label into something resembling a treasure map across a page or a screen that doesn't exist on a family road trip. You can talk about why people started using leet speak, who used it first, and what it reveals about how digital culture evolves.

Of course the everyday shorthand of texting has its own quirky world. LOL, BRB, and OMG are not just letters; they are social rituals. They compress tone into a handful of characters and carry emotional weight that would otherwise need paragraphs. The fun in these is not to emulate modern texting as a dry habit, but to understand how tone travels through language. On a ride, you can create your own family shorthand, a micro-dictionary of inside jokes. Use it to label things in the car, to signal the best seat in the back, or to identify the next rest stop with a single clever word. The game becomes an ongoing collaboration—everyone contributes a new term, and the dictionary grows with every trip.

Slang shifts quickly, which is part of the charm. A term that feels fresh today can sound squeaky tomorrow. The backseat becomes a living, breathing workshop where kids try out new words, test their sense of humor, and debate which slang will stand the test of time in the family's own linguistic archive. The mission is not to imitate a trend but to understand how language reflects culture and mood. The car ride becomes a laboratory for words, a place where every new term is a tiny hypothesis about who we are and how we want to be together on the road.

The ultimate takeaway is playful curiosity. Codes and slang are not barriers; they are bridges that connect people across ages, backgrounds, and moments on the road. They invite learning, but they do not demand it. They invite sharing, but they do not require perfection. In the backseat, the best codes are the ones that everyone can crack, expand, and enjoy as a part of family memory. So try inventing your own code, keep a notebook or a voice memo, and watch a simple car ride turn into a treasure hunt of language where every new phrase is a clue and every laugh is a reward.

12

SCHOOL ISN'T BORING WHEN THE FACTS ARE THIS WEIRD

Math That Feels Like Magic

Beneath the hum of the car, math suddenly feels like a magic show. Numbers become tricks you can perform with your hands, your memory, and a quick wink to the person riding shotgun. This section is a mini pop quiz for the brain—no stress, lots of giggles, and plenty of "wait, what?" moments that make the miles vanish a touch faster.

First, the nine-finger trick. It's the kind of math that earns a chorus of oohs and a few improvised claps from the backseat. To do it, hold up both hands in front of you and imagine you've labeled each finger with the numbers 1 through 9 from left to right. When you multiply any number from 1 to 9 by 9, you simply fold down the finger that corresponds to that multiplier. The fingers to the left of the folded one show the tens, and the fingers to the right show the ones. For example, if you're multiplying 9 by 7, you fold down the seventh finger. That leaves six fingers standing on the left and three on the right, forming 63. It looks like magic, but it's just a tidy little pattern in the digits that your brain recognizes instantly after a couple of tries.

Then there's the 1089 trick, the classic "math fairy tale" you can tell on the road to impress everyone who thinks math is boring. Pick any three-digit number where the first and last digits differ by at least two. Take that number, flip its digits around to create a new number, and subtract the smaller from the larger. Take the result, reverse its digits, and add it to itself. The result? A single number that always appears: 1089. For example, take 732. Reverse it to 237. Subtract 732 − 237 = 495. Now reverse 495 to 594 and add: 495 + 594 = 1089. It works every time, and you can do it with a little explanation for the rest of the car to enjoy. It's not magic; it's a trick with a dependable decimal dance that promises a small, satisfying payoff.

A quick, crowd-pleasing pattern is the multiplication-by-11 trick, useful for two-digit numbers and a bit of mental gymnastics. For a number like 37, multiplying by 11 yields 407. Here's the why in a sentence: the digits of the two-digit number, 3 and 7, create the result by placing their sum in the middle. So, 37 × 11 becomes 3 (3+7) 7, which is 3 10 7. Since 10 isn't a single digit, you carry the 1 to the leftmost digit, turning 3 into 4 and making the middle digit 0. The final answer is 407. It's a neat rule that makes people feel like you're bending arithmetic to your will, when really you're just riding the rhythm of place value.

A few more tiny mental morsels can keep the pace lively without turning the ride into a full classroom session. One simple fact is that any multiple of 9 has digits that add up to 9 when you keep summing until you land on a single digit. For instance, $9 \times 8 = 72$, and $7 + 2 = 9$. Try $9 \times 14 = 126$; $1 + 2 + 6 = 9$. It's a tiny, luminous trick you can drop into a conversation to spark a quick wow moment.

If you're aiming for a little demonstrable magic, the "trick your friends into thinking you're a human calculator" routine lands nicely here. You can propose a small, friendly challenge: pick a two-digit number, multiply by 3 in your head, then add the digits of the result. You'll find the sum is a multiple of 3 every time. Or pick any two-digit number, double it, add eight, and halve the result; the final number is always ten more than the original two-digit number. These aren't complicated, but they feel like secret knowledge that makes the backseat audience lean in a little closer.

Finally, a quick set of prompts that transforms into a game rather than a lecture. The driver calls out a number, and the passengers quick-fire a mental math trick that could work for that specific case. The first one to land a correct trick earns a little, friendly bragging rights. The goal isn't to win trophies; it's to make the brain hum and the mouth stay engaged. The more you mix up the tricks, the more the ride feels collaborative, a tiny, goofy classroom that never closes.

The math in this chapter isn't about long, sterile calculations. It's about seeing patterns, inviting curiosity, and turning routine numbers into tiny moments of wonder. The moment you turn a simple multiplication into a party trick, you've shown that school doesn't have to be a place you endure. It can be a toolkit you carry with you, ready to whip out whenever the car slows to a whisper or the radio goes to static. The goal is a memory you'll revisit later with a smile, not a dull ache you try to forget.

So tuck these tricks away, share them, and coax more out of a handful of digits. The facts aren't changing; your perspective is. And that shift—a little sparkle in something ordinary—just might make the next road trip the best one yet.

Science Class Plot Twists

The car becomes a rolling science lab when curiosity takes the wheel. On a ride, the world outside can flip your assumptions on their heads with a few well-chosen facts and a short moment of wonder. This section is designed to feel like a mini science show in progress, full of quick explanations that are easy to picture, easy to remember, and easy to share aloud.

Let's start with a few counterintuitive truths that often surprise listeners. Ice is not merely water that forgot how to be liquid; it's water behaving in a way that seems almost magical. Ice floats because it's less dense than liquid water. That tiny difference—one word, one property—keeps lakes from freezing all the way through in winter in many places and leads to a lively, dynamic ecosystem under the surface. Imagine a summer road trip when a lake is just a few inches away from the ice's edge, and you'll see the drama of density at work in the simplest of places.

Water has more tricks tucked into its folds. For instance, water expands when it freezes, which is why ice floats. That's how a chilly lake can keep life alive beneath a crust of cold crystal. And while we're talking about water's oddities, the temperature of the water in your car bottle can be a surprising little physics test. Hot water expands slightly under pressure and cold water contracts differently depending on the surrounding environment. It's a micro-lesson in how the world responds to temperature with a quiet, stubborn obedience to the laws of physics.

Two facts that flip classroom expectations make for great road-time conversations. First, Venus has a day longer than its year. A single rotation on Venus takes longer than

Venus's orbit around the Sun, which means a day lasts longer than a year on that planet. This is the kind of cosmic oddity that invites questions. How does that affect the planet's weather, its storms, or its rotation? Second, there are more trees on Earth than there are stars in the Milky Way. That statistic invites both awe and a quick mental map of scales—the forest of our planet compared with the vastness of space—and it makes the window view a little more muscular in imagination.

Turn the page to the familiar and watch it become strange. Bananas are berries; strawberries are not. It's a fact that makes kids tilt their heads and say, "Really?" The botanical truth is that berries have seeds on the inside, and by that strict definition, bananas qualify while strawberries do not. It's a small taxonomy twist that's perfect for a pause in the car, a moment to giggle and reread the label on the fruit bowl with a new sense of curiosity.

Lightning is another mind-bender. The bolt can heat the surrounding air to about 30,000 kelvin, a temperature hotter than the surface of the Sun. The air expands explosively as the bolt cuts through it, creating the thunder we hear seconds later. It's a dramatic reminder that nature loves spectacular theater, often in the sky above us, and it's a great prompt for a family discussion about weather, safety, and science in everyday life.

The sea is a never-ending source of drama on land, even when you're running it through a car window. The ocean's depths host creatures and conditions that feel like science fiction. But the fact that a surprisingly large portion of our planet remains mostly unexplored is what makes the ocean so magnetic for curious minds. You can point to a coastline and wonder what lies beneath, while noting how pressure, lights, and darkness shape life in ways that feel almost magical.

Sound, meanwhile, is a reminder that not every phenomenon travels through air or water. Sound needs a medium to travel; in a vacuum, as in space, there's no air, so there's no sound the way we hear it on Earth. That's why astronauts rely on radios and instruments to communicate far from home. The backseat audience can practice a little experiment that demonstrates this, too: whisper through the window, then switch to a muffled, closed-mouth whisper and compare how the sound travels in different environments. It's a small, tactile experience that makes a classroom truth tangible.

In science, the world isn't static; it's a constant series of plot twists. The easiest way to make this real on a road trip is to translate a fact into a question for the next rest stop: What happens when air meets light? How does a non-Newtonian fluid behave when you apply pressure to it? What would you see if you could ride in a beam of sunlight? These questions invite observation, speculation, and a little friendly debate. It's not about being right or wrong; it's about chasing the thread of inquiry wherever it leads and letting the curiosity pull the next mile forward.

A few quick experiments that fit into the moment without creating a mess or a hazard can keep the learning momentum alive. A simple non-Newtonian demonstration with a small amount of cornstarch and water on a twistable lid of a travel cup—tell the kids you're making "oobleck"—reminds them that materials can behave differently under stress. A short discussion about density and buoyancy can occur when you watch a leaf drift on a pond or a ripple run across a calm harbor. The goal is to make the science feel alive, not abstract and distant.

Ultimately, these plot twists aren't about turning a car ride into a laboratory designed for black-and-white conclusions. They're about turning everyday observations into conversation, questions, and a sense that the world is constantly re-learning itself. The car becomes a theater where science isn't something that happened in a classroom years ago; it's happening right now, outside the window, in the tiny decisions of the day, and in the shared questions of the people on board.

Famous Homework Fails

This chapter's look at school weirdness isn't about bragging rights for perfect tests. It's about moments when a mistake didn't end a project; it sparked an idea, a revision, or a breakthrough. The stories that follow are famous precisely because they started with a stumble, a misread result, or a wrong turn that somehow led to something for everyone to remember. They are the kind of anecdotes that make a car ride feel like a tiny, cheerful seminar in the art of turning error into invention.

The first tale is one we all know in science class: Alexander Fleming's penicillin. In 1928, Fleming returned from holiday to find a petri dish filled with bacteria smeared in mold. Instead of cleaning it up, he studied the mold's effect on the bacteria around it. The mold inhibited the growth of the surrounding colonies, leaving a clear ring that hinted at something powerful—an antibiotic. What began as a messy accident grew into a revolution in medicine. It's a reminder that not every failure looks like progress at first glance; sometimes it's the messy middle that contains the seed of a cure for countless lives.

Post-it notes offer another delightful twist in the story of accidental success. In 1968, Spencer Silver at 3M was trying to craft a super-strong adhesive, but what he created was the opposite: something weak, reusable, and just kind of "sticky enough." It wasn't until years later that Art Fry found a use for that adhesive in a notepad that could cling to surfaces without leaving a mess. The result? The humble Post-it note—one of the world's most popular office supplies, born from a failure that became a feature. It's a perfect car-ride parable: a small misstep becomes a tiny miracle when someone spots a use others hadn't imagined.

Teflon's tale is another lesson in persistence and misfortune turning into something useful. In 1938, Roy Plunkett was attempting to create a new refrigerant. A storage canister failed to give up its contents, and when he opened it, he found a slippery, platinum-coated powder that didn't react the way it should. The accidental discovery of polytetrafluoroethylene, later known as Teflon, gave the world a superpower: a non-stick surface that changed cookware, industrial processes, and even space exploration. The lesson here is simple: a failed experiment can conceal a functional breakthrough if you pause long enough to inspect the unexpected.

Let's talk about the microwave oven. Percy Spencer, after years of testing radar-related equipment, noticed a chocolate bar in his pocket had melted during a test. That small observation sparked the idea of a microwave oven. He wasn't solving a homework problem when the idea struck; he was reading the room, noticing incongruity, and asking, What if? The answer wasn't immediate, but once engineers chased the concept, food could be heated in seconds in a way that reshaped kitchens forever. This story is the sonic boom of curiosity—the moment a simple anomaly leads to a product the world uses every day.

The last tale in this quartet is Velcro, the fabric fastener that seems almost magical in its simplicity. George de Mestral noticed burrs sticking to his clothes after a walk with his dog. He studied the burrs under a microscope and found a structure that could latch and hold with the most mechanical, repeatable grip. The concept, refined through years of testing, became Velcro. It's a reminder that the best discoveries often sprout from paying attention to everyday annoyances—the things that make us say, "That's a pain," and then decide to understand why.

Famous homework fails remind young readers that failure isn't a dead end but a doorway. They're not about shaming mistakes; they're about inviting curiosity, resilience, and the willingness to pivot. In every case, the lesson is not that the world is perfect but that human ingenuity can turn error into opportunity, confusion into clarity, and frustration into something everyone can share with a laugh or a moment of awe.

As you drive along, you can turn these stories into a game with the kids: ask them to guess what the failed attempt became, what the original problem might have been, or which invention they'd try to rescue from a "useless" stage and reimagine as something valuable. The point isn't to memorize a string of anecdotes; it's to cultivate the mindset that ideas evolve, that mistakes are often steps on the way to discovery, and that curiosity is a durable fuel for any journey.

Quick Brain Boosters

A road trip is the perfect setting for five-minute mental workouts that sharpen memory, attention, and creative thinking. These quick brain boosters are designed to be read aloud, then paused for a moment of guessing, answering, or competing in a friendly game. They're short, portable, and easily repeatable, so you can stretch one idea across several miles or compress a handful of challenges into a single rest stop.

First, a riddle round that invites quick response. Riddle: I speak without a mouth and hear without ears. I have no body, but I come alive with wind. What am I? Answer: An echo. The family can try another: I'm not alive, but I grow; I don't have lungs, but I need air; I don't have a mouth, but water kills me. What am I? Answer: Fire. These two quick questions light a spark and then spark a discussion about sound, flame, and how we describe things that aren't living yet feel alive.

Next, a trio of classic wordplay prompts. Riddle: What has keys but can't open locks? Answer: A piano. Riddle: What gets wetter as it dries? Answer: A towel. Riddle: What begins with T, ends with T, and has T in it? Answer: A teapot. You can keep the rhythm by asking these three in a row, letting the laughter build as the kids trade goofy guesses and the grownups lean in to hear the punchline.

CRAZY RANDOM FACTS FOR CAR RIDES

A little logic challenge helps keep the brain in gear without turning the ride into a test. Riddle: If you have me, you want to share me. If you share me, you haven't got me. What am I? Answer: A secret. Riddle: The more you take, the more you leave behind. What am I? Answer: Footsteps. These classics spark imaginative thinking and a playful sense of mischief, and they're always good for a quick "What if..." conversation about how we count, how we remember, and how we imagine new uses for ordinary things.

To finish, a quick open-ended prompt that encourages collaboration. Prompt: You're designing a brand-new school supply that fits in your car cup holder and somehow makes homework feel like storytelling. What is it called, what does it do, and why is it fun to use? This prompt invites creativity while keeping the mood light and inclusive, turning a simple ride into a brainstorming session that everyone can contribute to.

The goal of these brain boosters isn't to test everyone's knowledge under stress; it's to create shared moments that feel easy and fun. Short, fast, and flexible, they're designed to be repeated on future trips, building a tidy tradition of playful learning that travels with you. The more you use them, the more natural it becomes to slip math tricks, science wonders, and playful problem solving into the daily rhythm—without screens, without stress, and with plenty of laughter.

13

TECHNOLOGY AND INTERNET WEIRDNESS (NO WI-FI NEEDED)

Old Tech That Looks Unreal

Ever ride along with the idea that gadgets from the past could only belong in old cartoons? Think again. Some devices look so huge, odd, or magical that you would swear they came from a sci fi film, yet they were real and proudly used by real people. Picture a room sized computer that ate power by the truckload and wore a path of blinking lights like a comet trail. ENIAC and its friends were so large that they needed their own air conditioning system and a dedicated crew to run them. The idea of a machine that could do math at lightning speed was thrilling, but the package was something you would probably mistake for a giant vending machine at a museum. These behemoths show how far technology has come, and how fearless inventors were when it came to turning a wild idea into a working machine. This is the kind of history that makes you want to lean back and whisper, wow, that was somebody's dream built with concrete, metal, and sheer curiosity.

Let us drift into the era of punch cards, where a single mispunched card could stall a factory line or derail a whole project. The punch card felt almost like a sheet of cardboard that carried the entire fate of a program in its perforations. It is strange to think that such small holes could decide if a computer would do something useful or do absolutely nothing at all. Yet there was a quiet elegance in that system: a human who carefully punched the right patterns could coax astonishing work out of a machine. This is how you learn patience and precision, the same lesson that helps you wait for a road sign to flip from a split second to a full minute and still keep your humor intact when the car finally turns the corner.

Crystal radios are another classic that might sound like a bedtime story from a techy aunt. They needed only a good antenna and a sharp ear to hear tunes using nature's own diodes. No power supply? That sounds like magic, yet it was a real thing that kids could assemble with minimal parts. The idea that you could listen to the world through a makeshift radio is part science, part mystery, and a lot of fun to imagine when you are miles away from the closest store offering a fancy gadget. When you see a crystal radio, you see a tiny reminder that curiosity can turn simple materials into a listening adventure, and it is beautifully free of screens and subscriptions.

Next in our tour are movie projectors, clacky typewriters, and the kind of telephones that look heavy enough to anchor a ship. A rotary dial telephone feels like a small art piece now, with its circular path that allowed you to dial by hand rather than by pressing a screen. It is a little lullaby of mechanics: you spin a wheel, a wheel screams back a tone, and a call is born. The first pocket calculators were almost space age toys, heavy enough to require a good backpack and a lot of curiosity. They were not the pocket computers we carry now; they were more like tiny calculators that carried a whole civilization through a long line of learning and trial and error. Then came magnetic tape. It was a magical ribbon you could wind around a portable case and press play to hear your favorite songs, stories, or school lectures. It felt like a magic trick until you hit the dreaded tape hiss, a sound you learn to love or tolerate as a reminder that the past had its own unique charm.

Old tech also wore another face: big, loud, and proudly analog. The light in a CRT television rests on your retina in a way that makes you wonder what a living room looked like when color first showed up. The screens were heavy, often curved, and somehow the glow of phosphor dots created a mood that is hard to recreate with today's flat panels. There is a peculiar comfort in thinking about a family huddled around a bulky set, waiting for a show and sharing the experience in real time rather than across separate devices. It was not just the devices that were different; it was the rhythm of daily life that surrounded them. The world moved slower, but the attention to detail was something to savor. A walk through this old tech landscape is like flipping through a photo album of daring experiments, all of them built on dreams bigger than a desk drawer and borrowed from imagination as much as from science.

An even bigger laugh comes when you find artifacts that seem to defy modern logic. The 8 track tape, the oversized floppy disk, the beeper that signaled with a tiny beep and a tiny screen of numbers, all paint a picture of a time when people learned to read devices with patience and a little humor. The drumbeat of progress turned these oddities into a historical museum of clever fails and brilliant saves. The point isn't to mock the past; it is to celebrate the spirit that said all of this can be done, and it should be done with a sense of style. The feeling you get when you see a bulky calculator next to a tiny transistor radio is the same thrill you get when you find a clue inside a mystery novel. It invites you to explore, to test, and to imagine what would happen if you turned a dial and discovered a new way to listen to the world.

In this chapter the aim is simple: to enjoy the weird charm of devices that once felt perfect and futuristic, and to appreciate how much easier life became once those ideas grew into something compact, refined, and reliable. You do not need Wi Fi or a cloud to marvel at these stories. All you need is curiosity, a willing ear, and the knowledge that even the most extraordinary gadget once wore the label of a dream and the promise of a better tomorrow.

How Stuff Works (In One Minute)

Technology seems like magic until you learn the trick behind it, and the trick is usually a simple idea dressed up in clever design. In one minute or less you can travel from a spark of curiosity to a working explanation that makes the world feel a little less mysterious. A crystal radio is not magic; it works because a primitive diode can turn an electric wave into a tiny signal that your ear can hear. The key is to find a path for the signal that does not require a battery, using the energy carried by radio waves from the air itself. The whole setup relies on the fact that the earth is full of radio energy just waiting to be heard, if you can tune in the right frequency and the right rhythm.

A tape player, by contrast, is a more physical magician. The tiny magnet on the tape stored information as magnetic patterns. The tape moves past a playback head that detects those patterns and translates them into sound waves. The trick is the audio signal being converted, amplified, and sent to your ears, all because a little magnet could remember a chorus of songs if you fed it with power and motion. A printer follows a destination oriented path: a pen or ink sits on a head that travels in an ordered waltz across the page, laying down dots that form letters and pictures. The dots are tiny, but when they light up together in the brain, they become words you can read. An infrared remote dances between the room and your device. A small transmitter sends a coded signal, and a thing in your hand politely nods and says yes, I have understood your command. It is the kind of quiet communication that makes a living room feel almost like a secret club where everyone speaks the same language of tiny lights and careful timing.

When you hear the word modem or see the blinking light on a router, a larger story hides behind the simple act of online talk. The modem translates sounds into digital data and back again, like a messenger who speaks two languages with perfect timing. And the slide projector, with its lamp and mirrored stage, becomes a traveling theater in a pocket of light, turning plain slides into a moving picture that dazzles the eyes. The lesson in every device is simple and powerful: complex outcomes often arrive through small, repeatable steps. A single idea is not enough; what matters is the relentless practice of turning that idea into a repeatable action that works every time. In this fast world of gadgets, the one minute rule helps you remember the core truth behind the trick, and then you can share it in a kid friendly, storylike style that makes a whole car full of air guitar scientists chuckle and nod in agreement.

Funny Tech Mistakes

Mistakes can be funny and teach us resilience at the same time. The world of technology is full of little slips that made people scratch their heads and then smile later. Sometimes it was a misread number, sometimes a missing instruction, and sometimes a human who forgot to press the right button. What binds all these stories together is the idea that clever people were learning what not to do as they tried to make complicated tools do simple tasks. This is where the best road trip stories come from, the ones that get louder with every retelling as the car fills with laughter and a chorus of Why did that happen moments.

The year that the human weariness of the Y2K scare became a global joke, a moment when millions paused and worried about clocks reading the wrong year. It was not a disaster; it was a reminder that people can plan carefully and still be surprised by small details. The big lesson is not fear but curiosity, the willingness to inspect a problem from every angle and fix it with humor, patience, and better planning. Then there are the little misprints that caused big safeworld booms. When a printer prints a message that seems to come from a different era, you might think a prankster has taken over the machine. But more often, it is a quirky set of misaligned settings or a misread font that makes the text look strange and delightful at the same moment. The team laughs, learns, and then corrects with the speed of a well practiced chorus.

One delightful example is a famous stage of video game history where a pixelated ghost moved in a loop and the programmers realized the shape of a wall forced a corner, turning the dream into a legend. The players stayed patient and the designers reworked the levels, turning an error into a twist that could be appreciated as a clever puzzle. Another tale comes from the early days of handwriting recognition, when a digital assistant tried to read a message and turned almost every sentence into a playful riddle. The Newton and its peers learned a hard truth that humans and machines take time to learn each other. These stories are not a call for fear but a celebration of the learning curve—the moment when a mistake becomes a better plan, and a joke becomes a shared memory that makes a car ride feel like a storytelling campfire.

What makes these mistakes so fun is that they often created unexpected, delightful results. Sometimes a glitch produced art or a voice that sounded like a cartoon character, and the people who heard it could not help but laugh. These moments remind us that technology is not a flawless hero; it is a helpful tool that sometimes takes a detour. The detour becomes a lesson in a friendly way, one you can easily translate into a family game or a quick reflection about how you would fix things if you were in charge of a grand invention. In the end, these stories are about perseverance, teamwork, and the ability to take a misstep, turn it into a moment of wonder, and then push forward with clever ideas and a lot of patience.

Some of the funniest tech misfires involve miscommunication across devices. A remote accidentally turning on the TV instead of dimming the light, or a speaker misunderstanding a joke and playing a silly sound at the exact wrong moment, turning a quiet car ride into a giggle explosion. These small errors create big smiles and a memory you can tuck away for future road trips. The takeaway here is that mistakes are not just mistakes; they are a doorway into appreciation for the engineering that keeps our devices humming. They teach us to be curious, patient, and ready to improvise, which is a handy skill when you are driving on a long stretch of road and the GPS decides to sing a different route just for fun.

Future Predictions That Flopped

If you look back at old magazines and early tech ads, you will find a parade of bright, confident predictions about the future. Some of these predictions are remarkable in their ambition, while others are downright funny now that we know what actually happened. The point of this section is not to poke fun at visionaries but to show how progress grows in steps. When you are in a car with a few hours to spare, it is comforting to know that even the best minds can misread the pace of change. Predicting tomorrow is a mix of science, culture, and a dash of luck, and sometimes the future arrives wearing a different face than the one imagined.

The dream of pocket video communication that would replace all calls seems obvious now, but it was once a stretch goal with a belief that the world would slide into near instantaneous, holographic, face to face contact. In many ways it did arrive, but not in the shape of a telephone in your palm. Instead we got smartphones that are smaller and smarter than earlier ideas could dream, and video calls that grew in waves, not a sudden flood. The flying car remains a symbol of ambition rather than a common reality, a reminder that transportation is a system of policies, roads, safety standards, and energy planning as much as it is a miracle of engineering. The dream of jetpacks becoming the standard commute is a story told in many living rooms, yet the reality is that science is often more useful when it works for everyone in safer, more practical ways, like better public transit or cleaner electric cars.

There was a time when every home would have a robot servant, a tidy helper that could cook, clean, and answer questions with a smile. We still do not live with armies of autonomous helpers, but we do have smart assistants that can tell a joke, set a timer, and order groceries. The future did not arrive on a silver platter labeled exactly as predicted, but the idea that machines could help with daily life arrived nonetheless, sometimes in the best possible way and sometimes in a surprising, imperfect echo of the old dream. Those misfits show the writer in you the power of imagination. They remind you that it is okay to dream big and still be grateful for what actually lands on your family table—safer cars, better batteries, and devices that help you stay connected when you want to be but remain quietly off when you wish to unplug.

Weather prognostication was another favorite of future dreamers. The idea of a tiny device that could predict the weather anywhere, and share forecasts at a moment's notice, sounded inevitable. Yet the weather is a stubborn variable, and early devices could miss a storm or misjudge a breeze. Over time, better sensors, more data, and smarter software arrived, telling us that predicting the sky is less a magic trick and more like a collaborative effort among countless hands, each of them learning a little more each day. The snapshot of predicting the future often shows predictions as a map with many detours. The fun part for families on road trips is to see which guesses come true and which drift into legends. It helps children understand that progress is a course with twists and turns, and that learning from wrong turns is a big part of how we end up with practical, everyday miracles.

So when you flip through old ads or imagine a future where every car talks to every other car, remember the core lesson: technology grows in steps, sometimes in leaps, sometimes in stumbles, and always with a human story behind it. The best predictions are not the exact ones that arrive but the ones that spark new questions, prompt fresh experiments, and push us toward better solutions. And if a prediction fails spectacularly, it is still a story worth sharing on a long ride, because it reveals the heart of invention: curiosity, courage, and a healthy dose of humor.

14

FAMOUS PEOPLE DID WHAT?!

Inventors with Quirks

Road trips are the perfect laboratory for oddball habits and genius minds to collide. In this section we spotlight people whose breakthroughs came hand in hand with quirks that readers can giggle at, wonder about, and maybe even imitate in small, harmless ways. These stories aren't about perfection; they're about curiosity, persistence, and the surprising paths creativity sometimes takes.

Thomas Edison is one of the most famous inventors in history, and his legend is packed with big ideas and a few memorable quirks. People often tell the story of him working late into the night, surrounded by buzzing gadgets and clattering glassware, and then taking a nap at his desk with a ball in his hand. The moment he dozed off, the ball would fall to the floor and wake him, supposedly giving him a fresh jolt of ideas just when sleep threatened to steal them away. Whether or not the ball trick really happened exactly as told, the tale captures a pattern we can recognize in Edison: relentless curiosity, a willingness to experiment, and an unusual relationship with sleep. In Edison's world, a crash course on failure was just another step toward a successful light bulb and a better battery. He kept hundreds of ideas on file cards, turning the world one spark into another spark of possibility. The mind that pushed the electric signal forward didn't always move in tidy, orderly lines; it zigzagged, revisited, and rebuilt until something clicked.

Leonardo da Vinci sits comfortably in the same room with Edison as a symbol of curiosity that never stops. While he painted the Mona Lisa with patient brushstrokes, he was also sketching flying machines long before humans learned to lift off the ground. One of Leonardo's famous quirks was his habit of writing and drawing in notebooks that often used mirror writing—text written from right to left, as if he was looking into a mirror to transfer thoughts onto the page. Why he did it isn't fully agreed upon, but the effect is clear: his notebooks feel like a treasure map, inviting readers to decipher clues about invention, anatomy, and landscapes that didn't yet exist. Leonardo collected ideas the way a crow might collect shiny things: he drew, measured, and pondered with a mind that refused to let go of a challenge.

You can almost hear the scratch of his quill as he mused about how flight could be achieved, or how a machine might bend light and space to bend reality itself. It's not just that he invented; it's that he insisted on paying attention to every subtle signal the world offered—so much so that his sketches read like blueprints for a future that would become real centuries later.

Steve Jobs offers a different kind of quirk—one that became a practical habit rather than a mystery. He reportedly wore the same outfit—a black turtleneck, jeans, and sneakers—every day. The idea behind this uniform wasn't fashion sense; it was energy conservation for the brain. By removing a constant source of decision fatigue, Jobs could channel his mental energy into the big questions, the product design, and the user experience. The anecdote is often cited as a reminder that very successful people sometimes optimize small routines to free up cognitive space for bigger challenges. It's a lighthearted example of how a simple choice can become a strategic tool in a life filled with complex decisions. In Jobs's case, the uniform wasn't just about clothing; it was a small rebellion against the chaos of daily life that crowded the mind of someone trying to shape the future of technology and culture.

Nikola Tesla stands out for a different kind of habit: devotion to precision and ritual. He is the subject of many stories about meticulous routines and a deep fascination with sensory clarity. Tesla reportedly found comfort in certain rituals, and he is often described as a man who paid extraordinary attention to the sounds and patterns around him. He also fed pigeons, talked to them, and drew inspiration from those interactions. It isn't common practice for most people, but it reveals a broader truth: genius can ride shotgun with unusual rituals. The point isn't that we should imitate every quirk; it's that the human tendency to find a personal rhythm—whether in a laboratory, a workshop, or a quiet room—can be a powerful engine for invention. Tesla's life invites readers to notice the rhythm of their own days and to consider simple routines that help focus attention on a problem until a solution emerges.

A quick note on context helps these stories land with families: not all quirks are glamorous, and not every quirk leads to a breakthrough. Some habits are charming, some are eccentric, and some are simply stories that remind us that great ideas often come through persistence, patience, and a willingness to look at the world a little differently. In these pages we celebrate the odd, the unusual, and the personal rhythms of people who used their quirks to push the envelope of invention. The next time you're stuck in a long drive, remember Edison's nap, Da Vinci's mirror handwriting, Jobs's uniform, and Tesla's pigeons. If these examples can coexist with world-changing outcomes, then a few weird habits in your own day could be the spark for something surprising, too.

Artists and Athletes with Strange Skills

When a famous name sits at the intersection of achievement and entertainment, fans often discover surprising talents that feel almost like magic—things that aren't part of the main story but add a dash of wonder to the person's legend. This section highlights artists and athletes who didn't just excel in their primary field; they carried hidden skills and unusual abilities that caught people off guard and sometimes sparked new passions in others.

Albert Einstein is a perfect starting point for this category because his life wasn't only about physics; it also included a long romance with music. Einstein learned to play the violin when he was a child, and he continued to enjoy it throughout his life. For him, music wasn't just background noise; it was a way to think. He once said that life is like riding a bicycle to keep your balance, and perhaps the rhythm of a violin string helped him keep balance in the long hours spent pondering complex equations. That combination—serious science with a gentle, almost poetic love for melody—made Einstein feel like two people in one: a scientist who saw the universe as a grand, musical composition.

Ludwig van Beethoven, another towering figure in music, offers a different flavor of strange skill. He composed masterpieces even after his hearing started to fade. The idea of someone creating harmonies and symphonies while listening with their ears in a different way is almost magical. Beethoven's inner ear could still hear the music, even when the room around him grew quiet. The result was music that carried a kind of resilience—sound made from memory, imagination, and an intimate connection to the structure of a piece. It's a powerful reminder that limitations aren't the end of a story; they can become the place where creativity deepens and finds new depths.

Mozart is another great example of artistry with a surprising edge. He wasn't only a prodigy who could compose at a young age; he was also known for his ability to improvise. When Mozart sat at the piano, melodies seemed to spill out in real time, as if he could catch ideas in the air and shape them into music on the fly. This talent for rapid invention—turning a blank musical idea into a fully formed movement within moments—shows how creativity can be spontaneous and collaborative with the moment. It's a reminder to listeners that inspiration can arrive in a flash, and the best musicians learn to catch it and ride it to a finished piece.

Becoming a great artist or athlete can involve many kinds of practice, and some famous names reveal a flair that doesn't always make the headlines. For instance, a dancer or painter can have an astonishing memory for sequences of movement or detail, a photographer might be able to anticipate a scene before it unfolds, and an athlete may possess a remarkable spatial awareness that makes split-second decisions possible. The key takeaway for families is not a list of unbelievable superpowers, but a sense that creativity often blends multiple strengths. The people highlighted here show that art and sport benefit from curiosity, discipline, and the willingness to explore unusual skills that lie just beyond the obvious path to mastery.

The combination of discipline and playfulness in these stories helps us see that the mind can hold many kinds of talents at once. If an artist can improvise in the moment or a scientist can play a violin to think through a problem, then perhaps our own road trips can become a stage for discovering hidden abilities. The car ride is a small stage for practice and curiosity, a place to notice the surprising skills that everyone brings to the journey. In the end, it's not about turning every child into the world's best violinist or the next Beethoven; it's about recognizing that human potential comes in many shapes, and some of the most memorable strengths are the ones that surprise us along the way.

Unexpected Origins

Remarkable careers often begin not with a grand plan but with a chance moment, a stubborn willingness to try, or a quirky detour that changed everything. This section collects stories about famous people who found their path in unexpected places or through unusual routes. The goal is to spark conversation and some "wow, really?" moments as you ride along, turning a long stretch into a mini history lesson with a smile.

J.K. Rowling's road to becoming the author of Harry Potter began with a delayed train ride. She has described how the idea for a wizarding world came to her during a long trip from Manchester to London. At a time when many people would have seen a delay as a nuisance, she let that moment grow into a universe of characters who would eventually travel with countless readers around the world. The origin is humble and almost cinematic: a moment in a carriage that sparked a lifelong passion and a book series that would redefine what it means to read a story aloud with friends and family.

Walt Disney's start in entertainment also has a story that feels almost cinematic. He faced setbacks early in his career, including a period when he was told he lacked imagination. Rather than accepting that verdict, Disney kept drawing, designing, and imagining new worlds. The lesson here is simple and powerful: rejection doesn't have to be the end, and a single spark of an idea can lead to a flame that lights up entire generations. Disney's way of turning a single spark into a studio that created timeless characters and immersive experiences shows how perseverance can convert skepticism into a lasting legacy.

The Google story adds a modern twist to the "garage start" origin narrative. Larry Page and Sergey Brin began as graduate students who built a search engine in a garage – a place that sounds almost cinematic in its simplicity. The garage becomes a symbol of possibility, reminding readers that the best ideas don't always require a polished lab or fancy equipment. Sometimes they arise from a shared curiosity, a messy basement, or a spare room filled with whiteboards and caffeine. That space became the birthplace of a technology company that would reshape the way people access information and connect with one another, illustrating how ordinary settings can host extraordinary outcomes.

Steve Jobs and Steve Wozniak offer another garage-origin moment that's become part of tech folklore. In a small space, they built products that people didn't know they needed until they held them in their hands. The garage story emphasizes the quiet power of practical tinkering and collaboration, where hands-on work and a shared dream intersect. It's a reminder that innovation often begins not with perfect plans but with the willingness to try something new, fail, adjust, and try again.

Harrison Ford's entry into acting carries a similarly unusual origin. Before he became a familiar face in adventure films, Ford worked as a carpenter. A chance encounter with a director who needed a carpenter turned into an invitation to audition for a small role, and soon he found himself stepping into the broader world of cinema. The story is a lighthearted demonstration of how odd jobs can become stepping stones to big opportunities, especially when timing, persistence, and personality align with a moment that can't be replicated.

Unexpected origins aren't about luck alone; they're about a mindset. They remind us that big changes often begin with small, imperfect steps and with people willing to take those steps regardless of the conventional path. You don't need a grand plan to begin; you need curiosity, resilience, and a readiness to try something different. Those qualities are as valuable on a road trip as they are in a career, and they give us a practical way to approach our own journeys: notice the strange, value the incremental, and stay open to the chances that lead to transformative outcomes.

Fact or Fib? Celebrity Edition

Ready for a quick, truth-telling game that fits perfectly into a car ride? Here are several prompts about famous people and their lesser-known traits or moments. Some are true, some are playful fibs designed to stump you or spark a friendly debate. Read each sentence aloud, and have everyone decide whether they think it's true or a fib. If you want the answers, you can flip ahead at the next opportunity or save them for a mini trivia reveal at the next rest stop.

Albert Einstein loved playing the violin. True. Einstein's relationship with music was lifelong, and he often spoke about how it helped him think. His violin was more than a hobby; it was a companion on long days of thought. The notes gave him calm and a way to reset his mind when equations grew heavy.

Steve Jobs wore the same outfit every day. True. The idea wasn't fashion-forward rebellion; it was a practical decision to reduce decision fatigue and keep his focus on big problems. The uniform became a symbol of his efficiency, a quiet signature of his approach to design and innovation.

Leonardo da Vinci wrote in mirror handwriting. True. This quirk remains one of the most recognizable details about Da Vinci's notebooks. It's a window into the way he organized thoughts and ideas—perhaps to keep his notes private, perhaps to tempo his thinking as he drew, calculated, and observed.

Walt Disney was fired from a job for lacking imagination. True. The story is often told that Disney was told he lacked imagination, which only strengthened his resolve to create worlds where everything was possible. The idea has become part of the myth surrounding Disney and a gentle reminder that early setbacks can lead to later triumphs.

Marie Curie's research involved dangerous radioactive materials, and she died from exposure related to her work. True. While the science was groundbreaking and important, the dangers of radiation were not fully understood at the time. Curie's dedication to science came with real personal costs, and her legacy paved the way for safer research practices and new treatments.

Katy Perry wrote her first hit record while balancing gigs as a rock singer. Fib. While she became a pop sensation with many hits, the idea that her first big breakthrough occurred while performing as a rock singer is not part of the documented path that led to her later fame.

Oprah Winfrey's first job was as a local news anchor. True. Oprah began her career in television in local news and continued to climb, ultimately becoming one of the most influential media figures in the world. Her early work in front of the camera laid a path toward a broader stage where she could share stories with millions of viewers.

Nikola Tesla could recite stories or poems from memory while performing long experiments. Fib. While Tesla was known for many fascinating habits and talents, there isn't a widely accepted record of him reciting poetry mid experiments as a standard practice. This is the kind of playful rumor that can make for fun discussion but isn't part of his documented routine.

Thomas Edison created the first practical electric light bulb. Fib. Edison improved and popularized a practical version of the electric light bulb, but the full invention was the result of contributions from multiple inventors over time. Presenting it as a single-person invention helps keep the narrative accurate while still delivering a lively mystery for your readers to unpack.

If you want, you can pause here and try to categorize these prompts by which ones you think are definitely true, which are likely true, and which feel a bit too tidy to be completely honest. The purpose of this game isn't to win or lose; it's to encourage curiosity, discussion, and a lighthearted sense of discovery. You can always come back to this section later and compare your notes with a quick set of answers, or save the reveal for a final "gotcha" moment at the end of the ride. Either way, you've turned a simple drive into a lively, learning-filled journey that your kids are sure to remember.

15

ANIMALS VS. HUMANS: WHO WINS?

Speed Showdowns

On long road trips, speed isn't just a number on a dashboard—it's a playful showdown between athletes who practice their skills 24/7 in the wild and humans who practice their speed in gym lanes and on tracks. In this section we stage three friendly competitions: ground sprinting, aerial flight, and water sprinting. Each contest highlights a different kind of natural engineering—spine, wings, and fins—so the winner depends on how you measure victory.

First, the ground sprint. If we lined up a cheetah, a pronghorn, an ostrich, and Usain Bolt for a 100-meter dash, the scene would look like a physics problem with fur, feathers, and a lot of dust. Cheetahs, the living dragsters of the savanna, top out around 60 to 70 miles per hour. In a straight sprint, they cross the line in just a few heartbeats, a blur of golden speed that makes the human eye question the point of shoes. Humans, even the fastest among us, peak in the high twenty-mile-per-hour range; Usain Bolt's record sprint clocks in at a little under 28 miles per hour, but that's in the best possible conditions with training, wind, and a smooth track. In other words, Bolt would look like a plot twist in a cartoon next to a cheetah's opening scene.

Then come the longer-legged speedsters. An ostrich can reach around 40–45 miles per hour on flat ground, with legs that look like they could propel a family sedan. A pronghorn antelope tops out somewhere around the mid-50s, and if you've ever watched it run, you'll notice the way its body seems engineered for breathless acceleration and ultra-efficient movement across a mile-long sprint. The moral of this ground show is simple: when it comes to raw acceleration and top speed across a short distance, many animals outrun humans by wide margins. We can learn a lot from their bodies—the long, springy spine, the flexible joints, the way the tail or limbs act as stabilizers—but we're not built the same way. The car-riding version of this debate usually ends with a chorus of jokes about speed limits and the Heimlich maneuver after someone tries to imitate a sprinting cheetah in a minivan.

Now the air show. In the sky, the rules change because air is a different arena with different physics. When we talk about flying speed, we have to draw a line between level flight and the famous diving accelerations of birds of prey. In level flight, the fastest birds push through the air at impressive clip, with the white-throated needletail often cited as a contender for around 105 miles per hour in level flight, a speed that makes human flights feel like careful, wheeled strolls. Then drop into a dive, and the peregrine falcon turns speed into a sonic boombox. It can exceed 200 miles per hour in a stoop, a move that makes the ground look like a static poster while it streaks past. In everyday terms, if you had a race that included diving and level flight, the birds could be astonishingly swift; but if you forced the race to stay strictly at level flight or straight across calm air, certain swifts still outrun us by a mile.

And the water, the big blue stage. Humans swim, and our top speed in a sprint is measured at roughly 2 miles per hour for a casual swimmer and closer to 6 miles per hour for elite competitors in short bursts. Compare that with marine speedsters: sailfish have been reported around 60 to 68 miles per hour, dolphins (including orcas) around 30-something miles per hour, and even some fast tuna species cruising in the 40s. In a straight water race, the fish and dolphins aren't just beating us; they're making us feel like we're paddling in a different layer of physics. The ocean is not a fair arena for human speed, but it's a reminder that in each realm—ground, air, water—nature has found a different sweet spot for speed.

So who wins, and in what category? The answer is delightfully nuanced. Cheetahs win the ground sprint, the diving hawks win the steep air rallies, and sailfish steal the water show. Humans, meanwhile, have a different kind of edge: endurance, strategy, and the clever use of tools and teamwork. In a social setting, that makes us excellent planners for road trips—the kind who organize pit stops and snack breaks with almost meteorological precision—but when it comes to raw, biomechanical speed, the animal kingdom brings science to the party with some truly jaw-dropping showings. The real fun of this chapter is not declaring a single champion. It's turning the race into a string of debates the moment your passengers ask, "Who would win in a race between us and the animal world?" The answer is, of course, "It depends on the race." And that depends on where you're looking: ground, air, or water.

As you imagine these matchups, notice how the animals' bodies are specialized for their environments. The cheetah's lightweight frame, thick tail for stabilization, and enormous heart are all about explosive speed. The bird's wing shape and air mastery are tuned for lift, glide, and occasional meteoric dives. The ocean athletes rely on hydrodynamics and powerful tails. Humans, in contrast, blend endurance, problem-solving, and technology. We don't outrun a cheetah in a 100-meter dash, but we might outlast it in a long chase with a plan and a car along the way. And that's the core point: in speed, as in life, there are multiple ways to win—and many ways to have a lot of fun arguing about it on a road trip.

Strength Surprises

If speed is a party trick, strength is the one that makes you say, "Did that just happen?" In this section we lean into the surprising muscle power of the animal world and compare it with our own human ingenuity. The results may surprise you, and they'll certainly spark debates in the back seat about who would win in a tug-of-war between a panda and a pickup truck—okay, maybe not the truck, but you get the drift.

Let's start with bite strength. The human jaw is nothing to sneeze at in terms of daily chewing, but it's not the boss of the bite. Human bite force sits roughly around 150 to 200 psi on average, which is plenty for biting into a sandwich or a difficult-to-chew candy but not enough to confidently wrestle with some of the tougher neighbors of the animal kingdom. On the other end of the spectrum are predators built for crushing bite power. The saltwater crocodile can exert a bite force in the neighborhood of 3,700 psi, a number that makes human jaws feel more like a paper cut in comparison. That isn't just a big number; it's a raw force enough to hold down a large animal's skull and still have a spare appetite for whatever tries to escape. The great white shark, another legendary jaw, isn't far behind in terms of raw grinding power, with bite forces reported around 1,200 psi in some studies. These are not targets for an ordinary chewing contest, and they remind us how bite force scales with skull design, teeth arrangement, and the geometry of muscles.

Now consider lifting power. Humans reach for heavy objects using machines and muscle. Animals lift and move with their bodies' natural gear. An elephant's trunk is a multi-tool of power; it can lift hundreds of pounds, often cited as around 600 pounds, and do so with enough precision to pick up a single fruit or move a fallen log. Ants, those tiny contractors of the insect world, have an almost magical claim: some species can lift 50 times their body weight. Think about a worker lifting a forklift while barely bigger than your thumb—yet their colony can haul loads together that dwarf a human's strength in a single moment. It's a reminder that strength isn't just about raw force; it's about the right tool for the job and the power of numbers.

But there are freak moments that redefine what "strong" even means. The mantis shrimp brings a punch to the table that isn't just about breaking bones. Its strike velocity is astonishing, and the punch is so fast that it creates cavitation bubbles in water—tiny explosions that stun prey and can even crack aquarium glass under the right conditions. That's not just muscle; that's physics in a fist. It's a reminder that brute force comes in many flavors. In the wild, strength often manifests as the ability to apply a small but repeated advantage—like a spider's grip on a web or a bee's wing-beat precision—that adds up to outcomes that look almost magical from the backseat of a car.

Humans bring something different to the table: tools, engineering, and teamwork. We design and wield cranes, bulldozers, and pulley systems; we build machines that magnify our own strength far beyond what any paw or claw could achieve. In a one-on-one contest with a strong animal, we'd lose—unless we bring a plan, a device, and a crew. The moral here is not that animals aren't strong; they are incredibly strong in the ways that matter to their lives. It's that humans have learned to expand the meaning of strength by building on top of our bodies with technology and cooperative strategy. And that is a kind of strength all its own—in a road trip, it translates into clever workarounds that keep the car moving and the laughs rolling.

Beyond bite and lift, there are other jaw-dropping examples. The mantis shrimp is not a one-trick wonder; it also demonstrates explosive acceleration and specialized sensory perception that helps it time its strike with uncanny accuracy. The elephant's trunk is a living tool system, capable of delicate manipulation and heavy lifting in the same breath. Meanwhile, ants show what collective power looks like when thousands of tiny bodies synchronize. The animal world isn't just about raw power; it's about finding the right kind of power for the job and often using it in astonishing, unexpected ways.

The human mind catches up in the realm of engineering, strategy, and teamwork, proving that strength isn't only in muscles—it's in the clever and the cooperative.

If you're playing a road-trip trivia game, you can pose a playful question: which animal would win a test of pure stump-pulling strength, and which animal would win a test of clever-machine synergy? The answers aren't always about who's the strongest in a single measure; they're about who's strongest in the right context. And that, in turn, makes for delicious car-seat debates: the mantis shrimp's punch vs. a human's crane, the elephant's trunk versus a hydraulic winch, and the tiny ant that can move something the size of a toaster. Strength is big and punchy in the animal world, but humans have a secret weapon—our brains and our capacity to work together to overcome unlikely odds. This section is your invitation to marvel at the surprising ways strength can appear and to enjoy the playful, awe-filled debates that follow.

Senses That Put Us to Shame

If there's a running joke in the animal kingdom, it's that our senses are pretty good—until you stack them up against the true specialists. In this section we take a look at the field of perception and how animals excel in places we barely even notice. It's not about humility; it's about wonder. When you start comparing sniffing power, hearing acuity, and eyes that see colors we don't, you'll see why many animals feel like the ultimate backseat co-navigators on a road trip through the wild.

Let's start with smell. Humans have a respectable sense of smell, but dogs and other canids live in a world of scent that we can only imagine. Consider the bloodhound, a breed famous for its tracking ability. A dog's nose can detect odors at astonishing concentrations, and when trained for a particular scent, a dog can track a trail that's hours or days old. The numbers are often described in magnitudes—some estimates say dogs are tens of thousands of times more sensitive than humans, and some even claim much more dramatic differences depending on the scent and conditions. That kind of nose is not just a novelty; it's a survival tool that allows canines to find food, friends, and even their way home across large distances. In the backseat, you'll hear a lot of jokes about sniffing out fries at a rest stop, but the truth is that dogs' noses are the reason some of their wild cousins can locate water in the driest deserts and track prey through forests long after a human has given up.

The eyes and the light show in the animal world are equally fascinating. The world you and I see is a colored mosaic, not a black-and-white map. Birds, for example, can see ultraviolet light—a spectrum that makes flowers look like glowing beacons and helps them find food, mates, and navigation cues that we simply cannot detect with our own eyes. Eagles are widely admired for their incredible visual acuity; they can spot a small rodent from hundreds of meters away and lock onto it with lethal precision. But it's not just birds that have extraordinary sight. Cats are known for their ability to see in lower light and their excellent motion detection, which makes them seem to glide through the night. In some nocturnal animals, vision is paired with a reflective layer behind the retina called the tapetum lucidum that gives them a second chance to see in the dark, producing those eerie cat-eye reflections you've seen in photos.

Hearing is another realm where humans are merely competent listeners while many animals graduate to superior sound recognition. Bats navigate with echolocation, a sonic GPS where ultrasonic pulses bounce off objects and return to the bat's ears as precise maps. Whales and dolphins use complex sonar across ocean distances, creating a deep, resonant orchestra beneath the waves. Owls, with their asymmetrical ear placements, can pinpoint the exact location of a sound in almost magical ways, a feature that helps them hunt quietly even in near-darkness. And if you've ever watched a dog tilt its head at a peculiar sound, you're witnessing the brain's attempt to fuse sharp hearing with context—an effort humans do with some wonder and a lot of practice.

Touch and taste add their own twists to the story. The star-nosed mole might have the most extreme sense of touch you've never heard about—an arrangement of tentacles around its snout that feel out microtextures and vibrations with alarming sensitivity. Some fish have taste buds on their fins or skin, which means they experience the world in flavors we'd never recognize without a lab. Taste buds in humans give us a surprisingly broad menu, and it's funny to realize that dogs often rate the world's flavors quite differently from us; a snack that makes you grimace may be a delight to a dog, who treats taste as part of a bigger sensory event—smell, texture, and the sense of safety.

The overarching lesson is that the animal world has crafted sense systems that function like specialized tools for different tasks. Humans rely on a broad blend of senses that work well together, but many animals have amplified one or two senses to extraordinary levels. In a road-trip setting, you can imagine a dog's nose as a co-pilot, a bird's vision as a radar system, and a bat's hearing as a built-in weather radio. The debate this section invites is playful: which animal's sensing superpower would you borrow for a day of driving, hiking, or exploring a new city? The answer is personal, and that's the point of this chapter—senses aren't just facts; they're fuel for imagination and conversation that makes any car ride a little more magical.

To wrap up, the animal kingdom doesn't merely outperform humans in one or two senses. It redefines what it means to detect, interpret, and respond to the world. Our noses, eyes, and ears are impressive, but many animals carry out perception in ways that seem almost superhuman. The next time you're on a long stretch of road, look around and imagine the world through the eyes of an eagle, the nose of a hound, or the sonar of a dolphin. You'll find yourself seeing your surroundings with a renewed sense of curiosity—and a little bit of awe at the wonders of nature's perception.

Sleep, Snacks, and Stamina

If there's one chapter in the book that feels like a road trip's afterglow, it's this one. Sleep, snacks, and stamina are the everyday realities that shape how animals and humans live, recover, and keep going through a long day on the road. In this final section we explore the rhythms of rest, the quirks of appetite, and the surprising ways living beings pace themselves for the long haul.

Sleep is the quiet engine behind a body's efficiency. Some animals sleep a lot—sloths and koalas are famous for their long daily slumbers, sometimes clocking in 15 to 20 hours of rest. Cats drift between naps and bursts of energy, with 12 to 16 hours of sleep a day not unusual for many felines. Humans settle into a more modest routine of typically 7 to 9 hours, though many families learn that car-ride sleep schedules depend on the kid or the lull of a movie and a snack break. In the ocean's depths, certain creatures practice a different kind of rest—dolphins and some whales allow one hemisphere of their brain to sleep while the other remains alert enough to surface for air. The image of a mammal half-asleep at the wheel of a ship has a certain absurd charm, but it's also a reminder that rest comes in many clever forms across the animal kingdom.

Snacks and energy demand are another great source of wonder. The daily calorie budgets between a hummingbird and a blue whale are like two different galaxies. Hummingbirds sprint on tiny fuel tanks, sipping nectar so constantly that their tiny hearts might pound thousands of times a minute. Blue whales, by contrast, gorge on krill during feeding seasons, taking in enormous amounts of energy to fuel their long migrations. The jokes about road-trip snacks become a stage for real science here: metabolism, energy allocation, and feeding strategies shape not just appetite but behavior. Some animals feast in bursts, then fast for long stretches as a survival tactic. Others rely on steady grazing or constant foraging that turns the long drive into a rolling buffet of opportunities.

Stamina is the final layer of this trio. Humans are famously persistent runners, walkers, and endurance athletes when the challenge is laid out. We've learned to pace our bodies, to hydrate, to manage heat and cold, and to use teamwork to keep going. The animal kingdom offers equally compelling endurance stories. Arctic birds undertake migrations that would terrify most wanderers, while camels navigate desert runs with remarkable tolerance for heat and dehydration. Tigers and wolves travel long distances in packs, not as solo athletes but as a team with shared responsibilities and strategic rest. The most amusing idea here is to imagine a cross-country relay: could a team of animals trained by humans beat a human team with the right planning? The answer would almost certainly depend on the course, the weather, and the strength of the snacks available along the way.

In the end, Sleep, Snacks, and Stamina is about rhythm. Some creatures rest deeply and rarely, others nap at every rest stop, and most humans fall somewhere in between. On a road trip, you can convert these rhythms into games. See how many minutes you can go without yawning, or guess how many snacks it would take to power a certain distance. The point is not just to learn facts; it's to notice how resting behavior, eating patterns, and endurance shape the way we live and move. And if you ever doubt how cool this is, remember that a single study on the migratory routes of birds can reveal a lifetime's worth of travel inspiration—and tomorrow's family vacation plans.

16

GROSS FACTS (BUT NOT TOO GROSS)

Sticky, Slimy, and Strange

If you've ever touched something that felt like it was plotting to stick to your fingers, you've met nature's own version of a sticky joke. Sticky, slimy, and strange are not just bathroom words you whisper to avoid laughter; they're everyday tools that creatures use to survive, hide, and get from one place to another. Think of slime as a versatile secret agent of the natural world, proving that goo can be useful, protective, and even funny in the right moment. In the wild, goo isn't just gross—it's a splash of chemistry, biology, and clever design hacking its way into the daily lives of plants and animals.

Let's start with slime molds, the kind of organisms that look like orange jelly perched on a decaying log and act a lot like a tiny, brainy team. They don't have brains, at least not in the way we think about brains, but they can solve simple mazes and optimize their paths to food sources. Imagine a network of slimy roads where every little blob shares what it knows. When you drive past a log on the side of the road and notice a glimmer of goo, you might be looking at a living demonstration of effort without a single muscle moving—just a smart, slow, slime-powered scout party.

Sap and resin are sticky friends of trees. When a pine or a maple is under attack by bugs or injured by wind, it oozes resin and sap that traps intruders and seals the wound. It's not just a sticky trap; it's a tiny medical kit. The sap clings to insects and helps the tree recover, and in the forest, you'll sometimes see droplets shine like glass in the sunlight. Those droplets are more than pretty; they're protection in liquid form, a reminder that stickiness can be a lifesaver.

The world loves glue. Spider silk is famously strong, and the droplets that coat many spider webs act like tiny glue factories. The glue becomes stickier as the dew dries, and the web shudders with the little jittery life of a morning breeze. It's not a messy, gross glue; it's a precise, delicate adhesive designed to catch prey without catching the spider itself in the process. If you've ever walked through a spider's web and done your best impression of a ninja to avoid becoming a snack for a bug, you've felt the power of that sticky science up close.

Then there are the slick, slippery secrets of slime from the animal kingdom. Snails and slugs leave a trail of mucus that helps them glide. This isn't just yuck; it's a well-practiced method that reduces friction and lets a slow traveler inch forward with dignity. The slime is a tiny underwater-like river on land, a slippery path that keeps their bodies from sticking to rough surfaces and from drying out under the sun. It's a reminder that even goo can be a practical prop in the daily journey of life.

Spittlebugs offer a cheeky, foamy disguise that hides delicate nymphs from hungry eyes. What looks like a gob of froth on a stem is actually a protective bubble bath that keeps young insects safe from predators and drying winds. The foam is composed of little bubbles that act like a sunscreen and a shield, a temporary fortification that makes the world seem larger and more confusing to would-be eaters. If you've ever played with a bottle of bubbles and pretended you were blowing up a tiny fortress, you've already touched a bit of nature's engineering magic.

All of these sticky, slimy, and strange things point to a single, simple idea: the natural world uses goo as a tool. It turns the uncomfortable into the useful, the messy into the strategic, and the sticky into a solution that allows life to keep moving forward. The next time you reach for a napkin after a quick road-trip snack, remember that being sticky isn't always a bad thing—it can be a life hack you didn't even notice until now.

Weird Animal Hygiene

Animal hygiene isn't just about keeping clean for the sake of cleanliness; it's about surviving in a world full of dirt, parasites, and unpredictable weather. You'll meet creatures that treat hygiene like a ritual, turning grooming into a daily act of defense and comfort. When we talk about weird hygiene, we're celebrating clever, sometimes bizarre, and always practical routines that help animals stay healthy in surprising ways.

Preening is a classic example. Birds use their beaks to spread oil from their preen gland across their feathers. That oil creates a waterproof coat that keeps them warm and buoyant, and it also helps shed water in rainstorms. It's not just maintenance; it's a tiny, efficient form of armor. A well-oiled plumage can make the difference between a chilly day and a day spent dry and sunny on a branch somewhere in the wild.

Dust bathing is another oddball hygiene hero. Elephants fling dust and mud onto their skin to create a protective barrier from sun and parasites. Camels roll in dust to reduce the temperature of their skin and to dislodge pests that would otherwise cause trouble in the heat. Dust can be a natural sunscreen and a parasite deterrent all in one, a temporary coat that insects and bacteria find hard to cling to.

Water is a frequent ally, and many creatures use it generously to keep clean. Penguins, for instance, take breaks from the icy world to shake, splash, and rinse, ensuring their feathers shed water efficiently and stay aligned in their tight colony life. Otters are famous for using rocks as tools to crack shells, but they also know how to wash and groom themselves with a careful, practical approach. The idea is simple: staying clean isn't a luxury; it's survival. Cleanliness correlates with warmth, protection, and healthy chances at finding food in a world full of hungry eyes.

The animal kingdom also shows that cleanliness isn't always about scrubbing until the world looks new. Some creatures deliberately roll in scent-marked materials to confuse predators or to claim a territory. Others rely on social grooming, where family members spend time removing parasites for one another. It's not a spa day; it's a team effort that keeps the family strong and the tribe safe.

Then there are the surprising cleaners among the smallest of creatures. Insects often carry out their own grooming rituals, using little brushes, legs, and tiny bodies to remove dust and debris from their wings, antennae, and mouths. It's a reminder that even the tiniest thinkers have a routine and a method that helps them stay sharp in a world that loves to complicate life with dirt.

As you listen to these routines, consider how hygiene is really a set of smart choices rather than a fix-all impulse. It's about balance: using water, dust, oil, and even friends to stay in good shape so that life can run smoothly from dawn to dusk. The animals in these tales show that cleanliness is a strategy—one that's as varied as the species themselves and as clever as any human habit you've ever adopted for health and comfort.

Odd Smells and Why They Happen

Smell is a powerful storyteller. It can signal danger, attract a mate, or simply bring back a memory faster than a photo can. The science of smells is about tiny molecules escaping into the air and meeting receptors in our noses, where the brain does quick, quirky math to decide whether a scent is friend, foe, or something in between. Some smells are sexy in a scientific way; others are downright silly. Either way, odors are part of how life communicates, from the roots of a flower to the backseat of a car on a long ride.

One unforgettable scent comes from skunk spray. It's a defense mechanism, a warning that carries a note so strong you could recognize it from miles away. The odor comes from a mix of sulfur compounds that cling to fur and travel through the air like a stubborn rumor. It's dramatic and memorable, a reminder that sometimes being a little gross is also a big deterrent for trouble. The science behind it is a neat demonstration of chemistry meeting survival. The spray can be breathtaking, in the most literal sense, and you'll never forget the moment when you catch a whiff near a forest edge or along a roadside ditch.

Another common stink is the familiar odor of rotten eggs. Hydrogen sulfide and other sulfur compounds are released when things decay, and the smell is a practical sign that something is breaking down and returning to the earth. It's a natural part of the life cycle, a reminder that even waste has a place in the world's big cycle of recycling. Easier to understand is the fresh, rain-after-a-storm smell, which comes from ozone in the air created by lightning and the sun's energy. It's a crisp, clean note that tells you the sky just did a major electrical performance, and it's a sign that the world around you is waking up after a shower.

Everyday smells also have stories. The scent of fresh bread or cookies in a kitchen communicates warmth and hospitality; citrusy notes from peels in the trash reveal yesterday's fruit's last party. For the curious kid in the back seat, these odors can become clues to a science experiment: what gases are produced by ripening fruit? What makes certain flowers smell stronger at certain times of the day? The science is vivid and accessible, a reminder that fragrance is not fiction but physics in motion. You can also find smells that tie into history, like the musky notes that once loomed over markets and streets as people traded goods and stories. It's a sensory scrapbook in the air, a way to turn a car ride into a walking, sniffing tour of the world.

Smell, though often underused in conversation, has a powerful social element. Flowers release their fragrance to attract pollinators, and human-made perfumes mimic those natural scents to evoke mood or memory. The same molecules that lure a bee can tell you a lot about a plant's life, a season's turn, and the way an ecosystem keeps its rhythm. Even the less glamorous odors have a place in this broader map: ammonia from a barn, the tang of sea air after a storm, the sharpness of a lemon that wakes up the senses. All of these odors have a purpose, a reason for existing, and a little science behind why they stick with us long after the car has rolled past the last mile marker.

The Ew Scale Game

The Ew Scale is not just a way to measure grossness; it's a framework for conversation, laughter, and friendly debate. Each fact you encounter on your trip becomes a moment to weigh it on a scale from one to ten. One means mild curiosity, a tiny squirm of surprise, and perhaps a quip that dissolves into giggles. Ten means jaw-dropping, eyes widening, and a chorus of mock horror that lasts until the next rest stop appears. The goal isn't to outgross anyone but to find the balance between wow and whimsy, to celebrate the strange in a way that invites everyone to join in.

As you read a fact aloud, let the room react. A kid might squeal with delight at the sight of a bottle of slime or at the idea of a fox with a soapy tail. A parent might throw in a quick memory of a science class or a joke about the sticky mess in the back seat. The back-and-forth is where the game shines: a friendly tug-of-war about whether something is a solid eight or an outrageous nine, followed by a quick explanation that makes the moment feel educational and entertaining instead of merely gross.

The rules are simple, and they fit in right with a family in a moving vehicle. Each person takes a turn sharing a fact and then gives it an Ew score. You should justify your rating with a sentence or two, describing what made your brain react the way it did. The reasons don't need to be complicated—short, vivid explanations work best and invite others to argue or agree in a playful way. If you want to vary the game, try a version where you also rate how funny the fact is or how surprising the science behind it feels after a short pause for discussion. The possibilities are endless when curiosity is the compass and laughter is the destination.

In practice, this chapter's facts become your toolkit for a quick, clean, and kid-friendly ride of discovery. The Ew Scale turns every mile into a mini science fair, every rest stop into a field trip, and every shared fact into a memory. It's a simple, repeatable ritual that helps families build a repertoire of backseat conversations that everybody can enjoy. So lean in, breathe in the fun, and let the sticky, smelly, and surprising world outside your window become the stage for the next great Ew moment.

17

MYSTERY PLACES AND HIDDEN WONDERS

Underground Secrets

Beneath the steady thrum of tires and the hum of engines there's a secret world that never quite makes it into the travel guides. It's a world of quiet tunnels, hidden rooms, and underground rivers that keep a city moving, even when the surface looks ordinary. As you roll along, imagine the ground beneath your feet as a layer cake of passageways, reservoirs, and stone that remembers every pedestrian who has ever crossed it.

Underground spaces aren't just holes in the ground; they're the city's oldest stories told in stone and mud. Some exist because a city needed better water or stronger walls; others were built as safety nets during war, or as experiments in art and architecture that decided to push the limits of what a building could be. The Paris

Catacombs, for example, aren't a secret tunnel system built for speed or comfort; they're an enormous bone library carved into limestone shelves, a deliberate reorganization of a city's crowded cemeteries. What started as a practical solution—emptying overcrowded burial grounds—became a legendary underground labyrinth that now whispers to visitors with a sense of history and a little bit of spooky drama.

Not every underground place is so macabre. New York's City Hall Station is a beautiful example of "you're not allowed to be here, yet you can"—a grand station once part of the city's heartbeat, now a ghostly echo that appears in occasional tours. It's not a dungeon; it's a stage set from another era, where marble walls glow with old-fashioned lamps, and where the idea of a city's past can feel almost within reach as you ride past the tunnels that helped connect millions of people. And then there are the urban basements of daily life—the long pipes that ferry clean water under the street, the vent shafts and maintenance tunnels that keep a city breathable and safe. They're not bombs and booby traps; they're lifelines that quietly absorb rainfall, move dirt and sewage, and give workers the space to repair, replace, and dream up bigger systems.

Caves form a different kind of underground library. In many places, cavern systems hide under hills or beneath coastlines, their ceilings studded with stalactites like natural chandeliers. Some are known by hikers and spelunkers, while others sit tucked away behind private farms or within protected national parks. The way these caverns fill with water, glow with bioluminescent organisms, or echo the drip of a lonely mineral spring feels like stepping into a different planet—one that shares a surface, but lives in a different depth. Even in cities, you can stumble upon hidden spaces shaped by ancient rivers and shifting sands. A tunnel past a rusted grate might lead to a storage chamber once used to hoard grain during famine, or to a quiet passage that connected old neighborhoods before modern subways came along.

One of the game-changing truths about underground places is perspective. What feels hopelessly old and forgotten to adults can be a playground for imagination to kids. A vent on a train line becomes a dragon's lair with a gentle story to tell, while a thick limestone wall becomes the spine of a friendly giant who once slept in the city's bones. The beauty of these spaces is that they invite questions: How did people decide to carve a tunnel here? Which secrets did they hope to keep or reveal? Who knew about them before maps and GPS changed everything? And what would you do if you found your own tiny tunnel that led somewhere you'd never expected?

To spark your curiosity during a drive, try a little treasure-hunt game with your crew. Pick a cavern or an underground space you've heard about and describe it using only three adjectives. Then guess what daily purpose that space might have served, or what era it belongs to. If you're feeling bold, pretend you're an explorer from a time when maps were stitched together from rumors and star sightings. The more you talk about these hidden places, the more your backseat becomes a launchpad for future adventures.

Underground secrets aren't just about the past; they're about what's possible when people dare to dream beneath the streets. Water systems that span blocks, tunnels that connect neighborhoods, and catacombs that tell a city's most personal histories—all of these remind us that the world isn't only what we see above ground. It's a web of hidden pathways, waiting to be discovered, discussed, and shared on every ride that rolls by.

In the end, the mystery of underground spaces is in the invitation they offer: look closer, listen for the echoes, and imagine the road you'll someday travel that might begin in a tunnel you could reach only by curiosity and a little bit of courage. The next time you're stuck in traffic, let your mind drift to those secret hallways and hidden rooms—the ones that say, quietly, that there's always more to learn just beneath the surface.

Buildings with Strange Stories

Architecture is storytelling through brick, glass, and metal. Some buildings aren't just places to live or work; they're narratives carved in steel and stone, each one telling a quirky true story about the people who designed them, the dreams they carried, and the mistakes they learned along the way. When you pass a peculiar facade or a tower that tilts the eye just enough to feel unsettled, you're looking at a page from a wider travel diary made of architecture.

Take the Dancing House in Prague, a building that looks like two dancers caught mid-turn. It's a celebration of movement and contrast—a new form wedged between centuries of Baroque and Gothic silhouettes. The design was meant to shock and amuse in equal measure, a reminder that cities aren't static museums; they are living performances that welcome new styles and fresh ideas. The story behind it is almost as entertaining as the building itself: a deliberate dialogue between old and new, between tradition and experimentation, between gravity and whimsy. It stands as a reminder that sometimes the most daring choices in design begin with a simple question: what would a building look like if it could dance?

Then there's Sagrada Família, a cathedral whose scaffolding reads as much a part of the structure as the stone itself. Construction began in the 19th century and has stretched into the present, funded by donations and the faith of countless visitors who see it as a living sculpture rather than a finished building. Its towers grow like trees reaching toward the sky, and its facades are a mosaic of symbols that invite visitors to decipher stories of faith, nature, and time. The lesson here isn't just about architecture; it's about patience and imagination. The creators who start something as grand as this don't always get to finish it themselves, but their work continues, year after year, welcoming new generations to contribute a piece of the dream.

Not every odd building is a cathedral with a grand vision for eternity. The Crooked House in Sopot looks as if it slipped from a fairytale into the real world, a lighthouse of whimsy that seems to tilt toward mischief. Its twisted walls and curved windows feel like a punchline to a joke about architecture, yet the structure is sturdy enough to stand for years, hosting shops and cafes as if the building itself is in on the joke. Nearby, the Crooked House's cousin in the kids' imagination could be the Habitat 67 complex in Montreal, a fantastical arrangement of interlocking boxes that look like a city condensed into a single block. It was built for a World's Fair, but it still feels ahead of its time—a playground for the mind that says modular design can become a sculpture and a home at the same time.

Other legendary oddities include the Gherkin in London, a tall, cucumber-shaped tower that breaks the city's skyline into a new rhythm. Its smooth glass skin catches light in a way that makes the whole street feel bright and futuristic, a reminder that modern design can feel almost like a science-fiction moment set in the everyday. And for fans of nature and narrative, Fallingwater in Pennsylvania is a house that seems to have grown directly out of a waterfall, a perfect marriage of landscape and shelter where the river itself feels like another room.

These buildings aren't just about aesthetics; they're about the stories they hold and the conversations they spark. Why did the architect decide to curve the wall this way? What story did the city want to tell with that tower's shape? If you could design a building that tells a story you care about, what would it look like? When you see a structure that seems to bend reality, you're not just looking at architecture—you're reading a chapter in a living guide to the art of cities.

As you drive past the skyline or pull into a city square, let curiosity lead your eyes. The Joneses' new favorite building might be the one that seems to defy gravity, or the one with a story as old as the street it sits on. And if your passengers start joking about a building that looks like it's alive, remember that humor and humanity have always lived side by side in the spaces we call home. The next time you're sharing a ride, point to a strange shape and imagine the conversation it started with the first draft of its blueprint. That's the magic of buildings with strange stories: they turn streets into chapters and cities into memory palaces you can walk through.

Borders, Islands, and Odd Maps

Maps are the closest thing we have to treasure chests that fit into your glove compartment. They show where things begin and end, where people disagree, and where a bit of whimsy once split a country into two pieces that seem to belong together and yet don't. Borders aren't just lines; they're long, strange stories about history, culture, and people who had to figure out who got what, when, and how.

One of the most famous puzzles is found in Baarle-Nassau and Baarle-Hertog, a place where the border between two countries runs right through a town and even through the doors of houses. Picture a front door that opens to the Netherlands on one side and Belgium on the other, with street signs and storefronts winking at you from different countries as you walk down a single block. It's a real-life maze, not a cartoon. Children love the idea that a building might belong to two places at once, and the grown-ups who live there have to know exactly which side of the door is which passport stamp. The effect is strange and charming, a reminder that borders aren't just about protection; they're about identity, cooperation, and the constant negotiation of shared spaces.

Vatican City and San Marino also make cameos in this chapter because they are tiny countries tucked inside Italy yet proud authors of their own history. They sit on the page like secret notes in a schoolbook, reminding us that the world is full of places where independence is defended gently, with treaties, ceremonies, and centuries of tradition. These two micro-states show that scale isn't the ultimate measure of significance. What matters is the story a place carries and how it shapes the people who call it home.

Borders can feel like a magician's trick when they bend or blur. That's part of the charm of our map world: sometimes lines move because of treaties, sometimes they move because of a river that shifted in a storm, and sometimes they move simply because someone decided to redraw a line on a plan. For a road-trip chat, imagine you could redraw one border with a friend. Which two places would you swap, and what new rule would you write for your imaginary line? The exercise is simple but revealing: borders reveal a lot about who we are and how we see each other.

Islands also carry the thrill of independence and the curiosity of isolation. Some islands are part of one country but sit far away from its main land, separated by water and time. Others belong to a country that stretches far beyond its mainland footprint, a reminder that a nation is a collection of many bits and pieces, not just a single block on a map. And then there are the "odd maps" moments—the kind of quirky cartography that makes you realize how maps are both accurate and imaginative. They can turn a simple road trip into an expedition across a patchwork quilt of real places and fictional possibilities, all in the span of a few miles.

When you travel, take a moment to notice the smallest border line on your route—the curb marking a street in one country, the fence that hints at a different zoning, the tiny island you pass in a river as the breeze shifts. Each one has a backstory that might lead to a future mini trip: a weekend in a border town, a ferry ride to an island, or a day spent tracing the contour lines of a map so carefully drawn that it becomes a map to imagination.

If you want a quick backseat challenge, try this: pick a map feature you've passed or seen in a book and tell a two-sentence story about how life would be if that border or island became a real neighborhood in your town. You'll be surprised how a simple line on a page can spark a whole new adventure, a memory a kid will tell at sleepovers, or a game you'll invent to test your own sense of direction and curiosity. Maps aren't just about locating things; they're about discovering possibilities, and there's no better classroom on a long ride than a map that invites you to wonder what lies just beyond the next bend.

Odd maps, enclaves, and island quirks remind us that geography is as much about people as it is about places. The lines we draw tell stories about who we are, what we value, and how we imagine our shared world. And as your car crests another hill and you glimpse a coastline that looks almost too perfect to be real, you'll know that every map has a secret heartbeat—a reminder that the world is big, strange, and wonderfully full of places that feel legendary even while you're passing them on a highway.

Legendary Locations (That Are Real)

Legends feel like bedtime stories we tell with our eyes wide open, the kind of tales that make a place feel larger than life. And yet many of the most legendary sites in the world are very real, standing as quiet witnesses to history, mystery, and human imagination. Stonehenge, the ring of monoliths in the English countryside, is one of the oldest stage sets we have for questions about the people who built it, why they carried massive stones across long distances, and how they managed to align the stones with the sun during solstices. For kids and adults alike, Stonehenge is a doorway to imagine ancient rituals, clever engineering, and the power of a shared dream to move stones and time in unison.

Far across the ocean lies Machu Picchu, hidden high in the Andes where mist hugs the stones and llamas watch over the terraces. The stories about why it was built—a retreat for a powerful emperor, an astronomical observatory, a sanctuary for priests—make the site feel almost mythical. Yet there it stands, carefully preserved by generations who treated it not as a fantasy but as a living classroom about Inca ingenuity, mountain geography, and the ways people adapt to extreme landscapes. The reality of Machu Picchu makes the legend feel both humbling and inspiring, a reminder that human curiosity can carve beauty and meaning even in the most rugged places.

The moai of Easter Island offer another kind of legend turned real. Somehow these enormous stone statues, carved with broad noses and heavy brows, were moved and erected on a remote volcanic island thousands of miles from anywhere. The mystery isn't solved yet, but the present tense of the moai is what captures the imagination: a society that built giant figures as a way to honor ancestors and shape a landscape into a memory palace for generations to come. The sheer scale invites questions about technology, labor, devotion, and the ways communities create meaning out of stone and earth.

Glastonbury Tor in England looks ordinary from a distance, but legends cling to its slopes like mist. From myths about King Arthur to tales of sacred springs and hidden doorways, the hill invites stories you can almost hear if you listen closely enough. The idea that a single hill could cradle so much folklore makes it a perfect color for a child's imagination—the chance that history and myth aren't enemies but neighbors, sharing the same street and the same night sky.

Then there's the fairy-tale castle of Neuschwanstein in Bavaria, built by a king who wanted his own palace fit for a legend. Its fairy-tale silhouette has defined how the world imagines castles, a reminder that architecture can create a dreamscape with practical walls and rooms. And the Ganges' sacred city of Varanasi, which feels both ancient and alive, carries stories about time, ritual, and a river's power to shape memory. Each of these places is real, and each carries a myth on its doorstep—two kinds of wonder woven together in the fabric of a single place.

The beauty of legendary locations is that they invite you to imagine, then verify. You can tell a story about a place that sounds impossible, and then walk into a real place and find the details that support or complicate that story. It's a gentle reminder that reality is big enough to hold myths, and myths are big enough to point us toward real adventures. The next time you're on a road trip, keep your eyes open for a hill, a stone circle, a balcony, or a fortress that seems to belong to a legend. You may not just see a place—you may feel a doorway open to a memory larger than the road you're on.

18

EVERYDAY STUFF YOU NEVER NOTICED IS ACTUALLY AMAZING

Why Road Paint Works

From the back seat, the road ahead can look like a simple, boring ribbon of asphalt. But as you glide past the curb and toward the next exit, the lines are doing a quiet, clever kind of magic. They are not just decoration; they are a made-to-predict system that helps you stay in your lane, pass safely when allowed, and know where the edge of the road is even in a rainstorm or a glare-filled sunset. The next time you see a solid line, a dashed line, or a crosswalk, you'll notice there's more to it than color and shape. The road is speaking in a language built from chemistry, physics, and years of testing on every highway you've ever been on.

Road paint is more than pigment and water. It's a carefully engineered coating composed of binders, pigments, and a special chemistry that makes the line cling to the pavement through heat, rain, and sun. A typical line starts with a base coat that forms the groundwork on the asphalt. Then comes the reflective layer, but the real hero is the thermoplastic resin that binds everything together and melts into the surface when heated. When a lane is painted, the material is heated so it flows and fuses with the microtexture of the pavement. The result is a line that sticks around through countless car tires and the punishment of yearly temperature swings. The science behind this is not glamorous in the movie-clip sense, but it is incredibly practical: a line that wears away slowly, night after night, year after year, yet still looks crisp enough to save lives.

The color is not just for aesthetics; it's purposefully chosen to convey meaning with speed and clarity. White lines mark lanes and the road edges; yellow lines separate opposing directions or mark warnings in changing environments. A solid line indicates where passing is discouraged or prohibited, while a dashed line gives you a momentary green light to change lanes when it's safe. The reason these rules feel intuitive is that they've been refined through countless hours of testing and real-world use. Subtle cues—line thickness, dash length, the tiny differences between a long dash and a short dash—are all tuned to be readable at a glance, even for a tired driver.

But let's return to the night drive. When you shine a beam of headlights on the road, you may notice something almost magical happening: the lines pop back, almost glow, as if the road itself were gathering energy from the car. That's not luck; that's retroreflection. The trick lies in tiny glass beads or prismatic coatings embedded in the paint or on top of it. These beads do not simply reflect light; they send it straight back toward the source—the driver's eyes—by bouncing light off their curved surfaces in a way that concentrates it back where it came from. The effect is most noticeable at night, in rain, or in fog, turning plain white lines into bright, guiding beacons. It's a small technology with a huge payoff because it reduces the chance that a driver will miss a lane boundary when visibility is limited.

In some places, you'll also see shorter, crisper lines that appear to shimmer as you pass, especially where maintenance crews have touched up a section of road. The shimmering isn't magic; it's the interplay between the road's rough texture, the paint's age, and the angle of your headlights. The more traffic that passes over a line, the more it wears, so maintenance crews batch in fresh paint and reapply the reflective layer to keep the lines legible. That small, quiet ritual—paint, bake, bake again, recoat—keeps the entire system reliable for distances you can't measure from the back seat.

As you drive, you may notice differences in line types that seem almost invisible until you need them. You cross a bridge, you peek into the left-hand side of the windshield, and you see how the line's edge protects the lane boundary even when the road allows a little shifting. You cross into an area with temporary markings for roadwork and you feel the air shift as the line changes from the familiar to a more provisional pattern. These changes are not random; they are deliberate communications designed for human eyes and human reflexes. And the best part is that they work without you needing to tune in —your brain does the decoding automatically.

If you want to test the magic for a moment without taking your eyes off the road, look for how the line contrast changes with sunlight. In the early morning or late afternoon, the line's edge can look almost painted anew as light hits at a different angle. In those moments, you can see how the road's surface texture and the paint's own texture interact in a dance of shadow and brightness. The road is a dynamic canvas, and the lines are the artists with a very calm, very practical brush.

What all this adds up to is not just a clever way to mark lanes but a portable safety system you can't take for granted. The technology behind road paint and retroreflectivity is a reminder that even the most ordinary stretch of highway can contain a pocket of engineering brilliance waiting to be noticed. The next time you pass a strip of white where the pavement meets the sky, give a nod to the quiet science that makes your drive safe, legible, and a little more magical with every mile.

The Secret Life of Rubber and Plastic

The rubber under your car's tires is more than a cushion that smooths the world into a ride. It's a living, flexible network of molecules tuned to grip, flex, and survive the harshest road experiments. The door seals that keep rain out, the wipers that scratch away at a rainy windshield, and the very plastic panels that keep the cabin quiet and organized are all part of a vast, invisible story about polymers, heat, and the clever tricks engineers use to make objects both strong and soft. When you pass a curb and hear the squeal that freedom sometimes demands, you're hearing a conversation between chemistry and contact—between the tire's rubber and the road's roughness—and the more you learn about it, the more you appreciate how everyday materials are engineered to do extraordinary things.

Rubber is mostly long chains of molecules that like to move and twist. The magic happens when those chains are cross-linked in a process called vulcanization, which uses heat and sometimes sulfur to create a network that stays springy but doesn't melt into a puddle under pressure. The result is a material that can stretch just enough, spring back, and maintain grip when it matters most. Tires are the crown jewel of this technology. They wear belts, plies, and a tire's own crown are designed to grip the road by creating microscopic edges that bite into the surface. The tread pattern is not a random decoration; it is a scientific page of information about how water, debris, and heat move across the tire's surface. When you drive through a wet patch, those little channels and voids become lifelines, shuttling away water and helping the tire maintain contact with the road.

Inside the tire, there's a whole ecosystem. Carbon black, a pigment that makes tires distinctly black, is not just for looks. It reinforces the rubber, protecting the tire from heat buildup and UV rays that would otherwise dry out the material. The air inside the tire matters as well—perfect tuning of air pressure changes how the footprint of the tire meets the road. Too soft, and you squish energy into the pavement instead of giving it a controlled bite; too hard, and you skip over little imperfections instead of gripping them. The balance is a result of countless tests and a deep understanding of how friction works in motion.

Rubber appears in surprising places beyond tires. The door seals, for instance, must be soft enough to compress and keep out drafts, yet sturdy enough to last for years of temperature swings. The wiper blades—rubber with embedded reinforcement—must bend without tearing and glide smoothly across glass, a trick that depends on flexible chemistry and the geometry of the blade. Plastic, a generic term for many polymers, keeps the cabin quiet and tidy through a family of materials that are strong yet light, flexible yet durable. The plastic panels that surround the dashboard and the headliner that cushions your ears in a long ride are designed to absorb sound and damp vibration while staying comfortable to touch and easy to clean.

But the real magic behind everyday rubber and plastic is resilience. You don't notice resilience until you realize how many hours of heat, cold, sun, and rough roads a material can survive and still function. The science explains why the drive feels smoother on a road that's poorly maintained when your tires have the right tread and the right pressure, and why a wobbly wheel or a squeak from a door can ruin a feeling of calm in a long trip. The everyday world is full of materials that look simple until you think about the way their molecules are linked, the way they flex, and the way they recover their shape after every bump. It's easy to overlook the quiet complexity of Mies van der Rohe's ideal of form meets function when the thing in your hand, or under your car, is doing something elegant in the simplest possible way.

If you want to see the secret life of materials in action, try a quick test while you're parked and the kids are buckled in. Press a rubber seal and listen to how it rebounds; then press a plastic bottle and feel how it resists compression and how its edges snap back as the shape changes. Think about the tape that seals a bag of chips and the way the bag's plastic film keeps air out. Each of these objects is more than a simple layer of material; they are a carefully designed system that makes a car ride comfortable, safe, and surprisingly clever. The next time you adjust a seat or roll a window down, remember the long, quiet science of everyday materials—the rubber and plastic that do the heavy lifting so you can dream about your next destination.

Sounds, Echoes, and Car Acoustics

If you ever ride in a car with the windows up and the world outside muffled to a whisper, you've stumbled into a tiny acoustic laboratory. The interior of a car is a resonance chamber, a space where every surface—seat fabric, carpet, headliner, glass—plays a role in shaping sound. Voices bounce around like kids in a hallway, but the car's designers tuned that hallway to be friendly to your ears. You may notice that talking in a car sometimes sounds flatter or crisper depending on the time of day, the weather, and the speed. That's not magic; that's physics at work. The metal body of the car, the glass, and the cushions all reflect, absorb, and scatter sound waves in specific ways. The engineers call this acoustic treatment, and it's a careful balance between keeping the engine noise out and letting voices stay clear enough to hear a story or a joke over the hum of the road.

One of the biggest culprits in car acoustics is tire noise. The moment you roll onto a highway, you begin to hear a soft, regular hum that grows louder as speed increases. Tire tread is designed to grip the road by creating many tiny edges that push against the surface. Those edges generate noise as they cut through the air and the rubber itself vibrates. The pattern of the tread—deep stripes, shallow sipes, blocks of rubber—determines the exact sound signature. Car designers respond by shaping the cabin with insulating materials that absorb those frequencies. The result is a sound that is not gone, but more manageable, a steady drone that doesn't steal the entire conversation or the music. If you roll down the window on a sunny day, you'll notice that wind noise adds another layer of sound, a rushing sheet that interacts with the tire drone and the engine rumble to produce a unique soundscape for that moment.

The glass in your windows also matters. Windshield glass has to be strong to survive impacts, but it also has a role in acoustics. Some windshields use laminated layers that dampen noise and reduce vibration. In premium cars, the glass is part of a bigger system called acoustic glazing, which adds weight and momentum to lower the sound energy that escapes the cabin. The door panels, the trunk lining, even the floor mats—all contribute to how speech travels inside the cabin. The seat cushions aren't just for comfort; they're dampers designed to absorb certain vibrations, softening the sharp edges of sound and making your passengers feel like they're in a cocoon of conversational ease. If you've ever noticed that a seat with a soft fabric muffles voices more than a hard plastic surface does, you're noticing a deliberate choice about how sound travels and how people experience time together on a road trip.

Sound in a car is also about how voices and music are projected within a small space. The closeness of seats means your voice can overlap with the voice of a child or a parent, creating a chorus that feels intimate and funny at the same time. The windows, when opened, alter the acoustics dramatically. A crack of air changes the curve of sound waves and makes voices feel more distant or more present, depending on direction and speed. That's why some parents prefer a quiet car for reading aloud, while others embrace the lively energy of the front seat where everyone can hear each other clearly as the engine sings along with the road.

In practice, the trick to a better backseat conversation is not to eliminate sound but to master it. When you notice that a line in a song sounds muffled, or your favorite joke lands differently in the middle of a highway, you're witnessing acoustic engineering at work. The car is designed to be a shelter from the world's noise while giving you enough richness to carry emotional beats—the squeal of brakes when something unexpected happens, the soft hush as you glide past a field, the shared laughter that rises as the conversation grows, all within a space that quietly balances safety and comfort. The next time you ride along a long stretch, listen for the difference between a cabin that feels open and one that feels contained, and appreciate the careful craft behind every decibel that makes a family moment feel real and memorable.

The Science of Waiting

Waiting in a car is one of the most revealing moments in the art of travel. It's not just about time passing; it's about how your brain experiences that time. When you're bored, time seems to slow to a crawl; when you're engaged, it slips by like a story that finally makes sense. The science behind this is surprisingly simple and wonderfully practical. Your brain is constantly taking in tiny cues from the outside world—the change of scenery, the sounds of the engine, the rhythm of your own breathing. When there are lots of cues, time feels busy and quick. When cue variety dwindles, time can stretch and drape itself over a dull stretch of road. The car's own soundscape, with its steady hum and occasional click of a turn signal, becomes a metronome that either helps time pass or makes it feel heavier depending on how you respond to it.

Boredom is not just a mental mood; it's a real cognitive state that lowers your attention to the present. In a car, that means you notice fewer changes in the landscape, and your mind fills in gaps with memory, which makes the moment feel longer. A stretch of highway with the same strip of trees, the same fence line, the same billboard can become a blur that drags on—unless you actively inject novelty. Here is where the clever, low-effort games of a road trip come in handy. You can find yourself playing I Spy with a twist, or try to notice five shapes of clouds, or see how many different shades of gray you can spot in a mile of asphalt. The trick is to set tiny, doable goals that re-inject curiosity into the ride. You don't need to pull out devices or plan elaborate activities; you only need to look with a slight shift in attention and turn ordinary things into data points for a tiny inquiry.

The science also explains why little surprises feel so satisfying. Humans are built to respond to novelty. A new sign, a different color on a toll booth, a roadside mural, a moment of humor overheard in the car—these little sparks release a cascade of attention and memory. They alter the sense of time by filling it with moments that become memorable rather than a flat, slow drift. When you point out a curious detail—a lizard crossing a highway, a curious shadow, a shape that looks like a map—you are not just entertaining the moment; you are building a tiny story that will be tucked into family memories for years to come.

In this chapter, we've learned that waiting is not a vacuum to endure but a stage where clever science and everyday imagination meet. You can shape the air of a ride by choosing to notice, question, and hypothesize about what you see. You can turn idleness into an invitation to learn something new about the world—about how the engine purrs at different speeds, how the road lines echo under your headlights, and how your own attention can transform a long mile into a string of tiny revelations. The next time you hear the car's quiet drumbeat or see a stretch of road that seems unremarkable, pause for a moment and ask yourself what hidden science is making that moment possible. You might just find that waiting becomes not a test of patience but a playground of ideas that makes the journey as engaging as the destination.

19

QUICK CAR-RIDE PARTY GAMES USING FACTS

Guess the Ending

Turn trivia into a quick, laugh-ready mini-mystery you reveal in real time. In this game you share a bite-sized fact and pause just before the final twist, letting riders shout out what they think happens next. The goal is playful imagination rather than perfection, so keep the endings silly, surprising, or delightfully offbeat. After a moment of guesses, you reveal the actual ending, which usually serves as a neat punchline, a quirky fact detail, or a tiny twist that makes everyone say, "Wait, what?" The format is deliberately simple: one person reads the setup, everyone else offers a guess, and then you close with the real ending and maybe a quick riff of your own. The car becomes a tiny stage for curiosity where facts start the fun and your imagination does the running. This is ideal for kids who love a cartoonish twist, teenagers who enjoy sharper humor, and adults who appreciate a clever love letter to weird knowledge. The key is to keep it snappy, keep it clean, and keep the pace brisk so the miles don't lag between laughs.

A good Guess the Ending round hinges on choosing the right kind of fact—one with a natural punchline or an unusual aside that begs to be expanded. Time your pause for maximum impact: a beat of silence feels longer in a moving car, so use that to your advantage. If the group is younger, lean into bright humor and visual exaggeration; if there are older kids or adults, you can lean toward clever wordplay or quirky, little-known extensions of the fact. Everyone loves the moment when the ending lands and the car erupts with a chorus of giggles, groans, and "I didn't know that!" moments.

Here are three ready-to-play templates you can drop into any road moment. You can adapt these on the fly by swapping in facts from your notebook or the chapters you've already explored. Remember: the aim is quick, stand-alone content that's easy to read aloud and easy to remember. So keep each setup short and leave enough room for a hearty pause before the punchline. If a round ends up with a favorite ending, you can loop back to it later by starting another round with the same setup but a different crowd-pleasing twist. The flexibility makes this game perfect for long drives, quick errands, or waiting-room moments.

Round template one centers on a surprising physical or natural fact. The setup is short and the twist lies in the story you tell after guessing—or in the actual ending you reveal. You might begin with a fact that sounds ordinary but carries an amusing follow-up you'll unveil after the guesses. The real ending can be a tiny but illuminating detail that reframes the initial fact in an unexpected way.

Round template two leans into historical oddities or odd combinations of science and everyday life. The setups invite playful speculation about what happened next, and the real ending often shows how weird history or science can be in ordinary moments.

Round template three plays with animal or space facts that have a clean humor hook. The ending you reveal should either multiply the wonder or flip the expectation in a gentle, kid-friendly way. As always, you're allowed to riff after the ending—add a silly prediction about what the animal or planet did next, or pretend to interview the fact for a quick sound-bite.

Sample rounds give you a sense of the rhythm. In one setup you might say, Fact: The octopus has three hearts, and one heart keeps beating even when the octopus swims —pause for guesses. The endings you reveal could lean into a funny implication, like: And that's why octopuses are excellent underwater marathon runners for the first minute, then need a snack break. In another setup, Fact: Bananas are berries, but strawberries aren't. Pause. For the ending you reveal, you lean into the botanical quirks: The real ending highlights that the banana plant is technically a herb, and the fruit grows in a cluster on a plant that isn't a tree at all. The punchline often lands as a tiny, truth-wrapped joke about plant taxonomy, which kids and grownups alike enjoy.

If you want a fast-start guide for the ride, pick two or three facts you know work well with a punchline, read them aloud with a dramatic pause, and invite guesses for a count of ten seconds. Then drop the real ending and riff for another ten to twenty seconds. Keep a light tone, praise clever guesses, and celebrate the silliness. If your vehicle has a loud engine or chatter-heavy passengers, repeat the ending once more after the reveal, just to anchor the twist in memory. The social payoff is simple: the more you play, the more you collect tiny, shareable moments of wonder—moments that turn any trip into a tiny comedy club of curious minds.

A few practical tips to keep the game humming: vary the length of the facts so some rounds feel quick and others feel a touch longer. That keeps attention from wandering and helps younger players stay excited. If a guess veers off into a tangent, gently steer back to the source fact and remind everyone to respect the time limit. Use clean humor and model good-natured participation to keep the mood inclusive and welcoming for all ages. If there's a tie, declare it a "round-robin tie" and declare the next round the decider. The real win is fostering a moment of shared curiosity, not a trophy chase. When you're ready, shuffle in new facts and watch the car fill with a chorus of "no way!" and "I didn't know that!"

To close this section, imagine the backseat as a tiny stage where curiosity takes center seat. You don't need anything besides a good fact, a quiet moment, and a willingness to let the riders stretch their imagination. The art of Guess the Ending is in the pause—the moment before the reveal—where anticipation becomes laughter. And if the ending lands soft and sweet, that's perfect too; it's still a moment of learning dressed in smiles. The next sections will give you more quick-fire tools that use facts to spark competition, collaboration, and healthy debate—without any screens and without slowing your drive.

True, False, or Trick

Falsehood can travel fast, but truth travels faster when you're in motion. This game is a rapid-fire round of statements inspired by the kind of bite-sized facts in Crazy Random Facts for Car Rides. The setup is simple: read a statement aloud and invite quick judgments from the car. Is it true? Is it false? Or is it a trick that blends truth with a common myth or exaggeration? The "Trick" category is the wink in the eye—something that sounds true but is either semi-true or a well-known myth. The aim is to sharpen intuition in a light, playful way and keep the brain buzzing on a short, shared timeline.

How to play in the car: designate a rotating reader who will present each statement with a straight face. Give everyone a moment to think, then call out their answer—true, false, or trick. A quick reveal follows, with a one-sentence explanation that reinforces the fact or spears a common misconception. The best rounds move fast, moving through a handful of statements in a single sitting. The quick tempo makes it ideal for a few minutes of entertainment between destinations or while you're waiting in line for coffee or at a rest stop.

The key to a smooth True, False, or Trick session is clarity and fairness. Use statements that are age-appropriate and easy to parse in a noise-filled car. Start with a few obvious truths and falsehoods to set the tone, then sprinkle in a trick that prompts a second thought. As players gain confidence, you can add a little complexity—slightly twist the wording, use a broader concept, or tie the statements to current events in a harmless way—as long as you stay within the clean, friendly domain of the book. If the car contains mixed ages, keep the content approachable, with extra fun facts simple enough for kids to understand but not boring for adults. The practical timing rule is to keep each statement under ten seconds of speaking and a single-sentence justification for the reveal; this preserves momentum and avoids a lull.

CRAZY RANDOM FACTS FOR CAR RIDES

Below are three rounds you can start with right away. They strike a balance between widely known facts and common myths so you can assess whether the group is feeling confident or needs a quick reset. For each statement you'll read it aloud, pause, and invite guesses. Then you reveal the answer and provide a crisp reason that lands the learning while keeping the mood light. Remember, even a false statement can become a moment of laughter and learning if you explain it with warmth and clarity. Round one might begin with a common myth that many people have heard; round two can introduce a little more complexity with a borderline truth; round three can close with something surprising enough to spark a "no way" reaction from the backseat.

Round one reads nicely to set the vibe: Statement: Bats are blind. Pause and listen for the verdict—true, false, or trick. The reveal: False. Bats aren't blind; they rely on echolocation and good eyesight, though echolocation helps in the dark. Briefly explain the science with a simple example, like how a bat can locate a moth by sensing tiny sound waves bouncing off the insect's wings. Round two shifts toward history and science. Statement: The Great Wall of China is visible from space to the naked eye. Pause for guesses. The reveal: Trick. It isn't clearly visible from the Moon or from most orbits, and it's not a single, continuous line that you can pick out easily without aid. Add a quick clarifier about how astronauts've described their views from space, and emphasize the difference between popular myth and astronomical observation. Round three leans into biology with a soft twist. Statement: Humans have more bones as a baby than as an adult. Pause. The reveal: True, because as infants we have more bones that fuse together as we grow. You can add a fun aside about how some of the "extra" bones disappear when you curl your fist or stretch your fingers, and how the human skeleton changes from baby to adult while staying strong enough to stand up to a long road trip.

Fact Relay

If you like word chains that spark creativity, you'll adore Fact Relay. It's all about building a tidy chain of related facts and questions, each one nudging the next in clever ways. The rule is simple: one person starts with a fact, the next person adds a related fact or asks a clarifying question that ties to the first, and the chain continues around the car until everyone has had a turn. The best chains feel like a friendly thread that pulls the conversation from one surprising topic to the next, with a laugh or a "wow, I didn't know that!" at each link. The beauty of this game is how little you need beyond your memory and a willingness to think on your feet. It's perfect for long drives when you want a cooperative, not competitive, mode of play.

To maximize flow, choose a starting fact that's vivid and easy to connect to another fact. If a link stalls, you can pivot with a bridging fact that smoothly ties two ideas together, or you can pose a supporting question that invites others to contribute. A good strategy is to seed the line with a theme—animals, space, or everyday objects—so players know which direction to go. If a player's turn arrives and they're blank, the rule of the game allows a short pause, after which they can pass with a small prompt, like "I'm thinking of a link to something else in this chapter." This keeps the momentum alive without awkward silence.

The first example chain might start with a striking fact about space: The Sun contains 99.86 percent of the solar system's mass. The next player adds a related space or science fact: It's so massive that its gravity tug is felt across the entire system, guiding the orbits of planets. The next player can bridge to physics by noting that gravity is a fundamental force that shapes both space and time, which leads to a natural turn toward everyday effects, like how gravity affects objects during a car acceleration or when you hit a speed bump. The following player might connect to biology with a fact about how gravity influenced early life on Earth, which then loops back to a curious animal fact: tiny creatures in gravity-rich environments might have different navigational strategies. As you see, the chain rewards creativity as much as accuracy, so lean into playful associations, and celebrate the quirky links between topics.

A second example goes in a different direction. It starts with a fact about a domestic object that surprises people—like how a paperclip can conduct electricity in particular circumstances. The next player expands by tying it to a basic principle of electricity, perhaps mentioning conductive materials in everyday gadgets. The third player might pivot to a related fact about batteries, fuel cells, or energy storage, and then the final player could loop to a surprising animal or space tie-in that relates to energy or chemistry. The aim is a flowing sequence of ideas that feels like a mini-lesson stitched together with light humor.

In addition to straightforward chains, you can introduce a light constraint to keep things lively—like limiting each link to a specific subtopic (for example, "choose only biology-related facts for this round"). Or impose a speed limit: each turn has to be spoken within two sentences, keeping the pace brisk and the chatter focused. If someone makes a brilliant mental leap, celebrate it aloud and encourage others to riff on that direction for the rest of the chain. The relevant takeaway is that the chain is less about getting every single fact perfectly correct and more about demonstrating curiosity, creative thinking, and the joy of connecting ideas in an instant.

Here are two ready-made chain sketches you can drop into the car right away. In the first, you begin with a vivid, image-rich fact that invites a natural connection to a science concept. The second chain begins with a domestic object and wanders through nature, science, and human invention, finishing with a surprising real-world tie-in. Both are designed to be easily explained aloud, with short turns from each passenger to keep everyone engaged. If a passenger is shy, invite them to contribute by posing a question or offering a related keyword instead of a full fact, so everyone can participate at their own comfort level. The most important thing is to keep the chain moving and the ideas bouncing around the car like ping-pong balls—fast, bright, and a little unpredictable.

Debate Club (Backseat Edition)

Backseat debates are a delightful way to stretch critical thinking and encourage confident expression in a safe, light-hearted environment. The premise is simple: a handful of goofy, fact-flavored prompts that spark friendly, quick-fire arguments. You don't need a formal podium or a timer; the car itself becomes the debate hall, and the passengers rotate as the players, the judge, and the audience. The driver or a designated person can act as moderator, keeping time, announcing the next prompt, and announcing the winner of each mini-debate with a simple, jovial verdict. The aim is not to "win" in a serious sense but to practice presenting a position clearly, listening to others, and laughing together at the quirks of facts we all know and don't know yet.

The art of a good Backseat Debate is in the prompts: they should be light, non-polarizing, and easy to argue from both sides. Short, punchy assertions work best in the confinement of a car, where attention spans are brief and conversations move quickly. Focus on positions that let kids explain their reasoning aloud, while offering opportunities for adults to model concise, respectful argumentation. Remind everyone to avoid personal jabs and to stay curious rather than critical. After each round, give the audience a moment to react with a cheer or a friendly groan, which reinforces the social warmth of the game and keeps the ride pleasant for everyone involved.

To help you get started, here are a handful of kid-friendly prompts you can deploy the moment the car hits cruising speed. Each prompt invites a stance and allows for quick rebuttals or supportive arguments. You can mix in prompts that hinge on everyday objects, famous people, animal abilities, or oddities from the book's chapters. For example, you might pose: Which is the better travel companion on a long trip—an animal that can predict weather via its sensing abilities or a device that can map out safe routes in real time? The debate invites explanations that are short, sincere, and sprinkled with humor. Another prompt could be: If you could rename one everyday object after a famous scientist, which item would you pick and why? The structure is simple: two sides, a short period for opening statements, a quick round of cross-examination where each side asks a clarifying question, and a closing argument that wraps up the point with a memorable line. The judge announces the winner with a light-hearted verdict, and you move on to the next prompt.

If you want a smoother flow with a consistent cadence, keep a few ground rules in your pocket. Each debater has a limited time to present—say thirty seconds for opening statements and twenty seconds for rebuttals—though you can adjust to fit your speed and the age range. The judge can enforce a "one point" reward for the cheekiest line, a "two points" reward for the most persuasive argument, and a final overall score at the end of the ride. You'll be surprised how quickly kids gain confidence in public speaking when the topic is light, funny, and backed by a few well-chosen facts. After a few rounds you'll see that debating about bananas, clouds, or sleeping habits of animals can become a surprisingly rich exercise in reasoning, listening, and humor.

These four game modes—the Guess the Ending, True, False, or Trick, Fact Relay, and Debate Club (Backseat Edition)—form a flexible toolkit for turning any road trip into a learning-and-laughing experience. You can mix and match within a single ride, or you can reserve one game for short bursts and another for longer stretches. Each game is designed to require zero supplies and to work in quick bursts, so you can play while the car is moving, while you're parked, or while you're waiting in line at a rest stop or airport. The point is simple: keep it fast, keep it kind, keep it curious, and let the facts do the heavy lifting while your voices carry the surprises. With these approaches, you'll turn every mile into a mini trivia party, and every "are we there yet?" moment into a moment of playful learning and shared laughter.

KEEP THE CURIOSITY ROLLING

Make Your Own Fact Jar

Your car windows frame a moving stage, and on that stage curiosity can perform a little magic. The Make Your Own Fact Jar turns everyday drive-time chatter into a growing archive of wow moments. It's not a classroom assignment, it's a family ritual that fits in a glove compartment and travels with you from grocery runs to long-haul road trips. The jar becomes a memory capsule, a tangible reminder that the drive isn't just a journey between places but a chance to collect tiny, shareable wonders. Start with something simple: a small jar, a plain box, or a pocket notebook that travels with the kids. If you don't have a jar handy, a stack of index cards or a few sticky notes tucked into the seat pocket will work just fine. The point is to have a dedicated home for the facts you discover, a place where every new idea earns a little stamp of entry and a story to tell later. The act of writing something down matters because it commits you to noticing again on the next trip, and it gives you a launchpad for conversation instead of silence when the miles get long.

When you set up the jar, you can make it colorful and friendly. Color-coded labels for different topics keep the jar organized without turning into a chore. You might use one color for animals and another for space, a third for human body oddities, and a fourth for history's quirks. The colors signal your brain to think in categories, which makes sharing easier and faster when you need a quick prompt during a lull in the driving. But color isn't the only trick. You can also create a simple system for what goes on a card: a short one-liner that captures the fact in a pacey, read-aloud-friendly way. If a fact feels long or clunky, you can shorten it into a punchy three or four word line that someone can riff on. The elegance of the jar is that it honors brevity while inviting imagination. The best cards are the ones that spark a grin, a gasp, or a quick debate about whether the fact is truly true.

The process of collecting is flexible and forgiving. Everyone in the car can contribute. If you hear something on the radio, see a sign at a rest stop, or remember an odd thing from a story you heard earlier in the day, you jot it down when you have a moment. You don't need to verify every fact right away, and you don't need to have the perfect wording in the moment. The charm of a family fact jar is that the real polish comes later, during a quick

CRAZY RANDOM FACTS FOR CAR RIDES

read-aloud on the road or during a pause at a stoplight where the car's hum becomes a stage for a rapid facts-and-reactions show. Verification can happen after the trip, at the kitchen table or during a quiet moment at home. The important thing is to capture the spark—the surprise that makes you lean in a little, smile, and want to share it with someone else.

To get the most out of your jar, make the act of adding a card a small, almost ceremonial moment. A quick ritual can be as simple as passing the jar around to each passenger and asking for one new fact or one curious question you'd like to answer later. You might set a soft timer for a minute so everyone has a chance to think and speak without feeling rushed. You can add a feature that makes the jar even more personal: a page in the back where you jot down who shared the fact and what made it memorable. Later, you can flip back through the jar and relive the road trips by reconnecting with the moment you first heard each idea.

Some families enjoy adding a little bit of playful editing. After a few trips, you can invite everyone to vote on which cards feel like the strongest conversation starters. You might keep a running tally of favorites, not to turn the jar into a competition but to show how your curiosity evolves. If a card didn't spark much discussion at first, you can revisit it later. The best cards often reveal themselves in the second or third read, when the memory of the drive is still fresh and the delivery is more relaxed. The jar is not a benchmark of knowledge; it's a celebration of curiosity, a portable scrapbook of moments that felt surprising enough to want to share again.

If you ever find that the car's energy dips or that the same few facts keep coming up, you can refresh the jar with a theme. For example, one week you might collect only space facts, the next only animal oddities, the next a mix of kitchen curiosities and everyday marvels. The constraint is liberating, not limiting. It nudges you toward new corners of your world—corners you can explore together on the road. And because the jar is easy to carry and easy to use, it travels with you to school drop-offs, to the park, to grandma's house, to the next family vacation. The value isn't just in the facts themselves; it's in the habit you're building. The habit is what turns a standard commute into a curiosity relay race, with every mile presenting another opportunity to learn, laugh, and connect.

As the jar fills, the drive changes. You'll notice a shift from chasing new information to savoring shared moments. The jar becomes a cue for pauses—a moment to press the brakes on screen time, take a breath, and listen to one another. It also becomes a bridge to broader learning. If a card invites a question that begs for more detail, you have a ready prompt for a quick after-dinner research session, a quick visit to the library, or a family-friendly website that you can explore together. The goal is not to master every fact but to nourish a sense of wonder. Keep the jar handy, keep it light, and let it grow with your family's interests. Most trips don't need a grand reveal; they only need a moment when someone says something that makes the car laugh or exhale in surprised delight. With a simple jar in place, you'll find that curiosity has a home in every ride, and your family gains a shared language for noticing the extraordinary in the ordinary.

Become a Road-Trip Reporter

The road is your classroom, and the backseat is your newsroom. Becoming a Road-Trip Reporter is about turning ordinary views into tiny reports that honor curiosity rather than polish it into perfection. This role is not about delivering a flawless monologue; it's about practice—the practice of noticing, asking, and sharing. The reporter helps the family transform travel time into a living encyclopedia of quick moments, each one a prompt for conversation. Think of the reporter as a captain of attention. They steer the family toward the next exchange, guiding everyone to pause long enough to notice something new and then to translate that noticing into words that others can hear and enjoy.

To start, encourage kids to ask questions aloud. If they see a strange sign or a peculiar landscape, prompt them to describe it in a sentence or two. Then invite the rest of the car to guess what problem the sign might be solving or why that landscape might exist. This is not a test; it's a conversation starter, a chance to practice clear, vivid description and a willingness to wonder aloud. The reporter can also play the role of memory keeper, jotting quick notes about what was observed and what questions arose. You can do this on the go with a phone note, a napkin tucked into the glove box, or a tiny notebook. The key is to keep it lightweight and fun so it never feels like a chore.

Rotation is your friend here. A trip might feature a different reporter every time, or you can designate a daily or per-ride role. The goal is to give every voice room to experiment with language and timing. Short, punchy lines work wonderfully on the move, so encourage quick one-liners that capture the moment and invite a reaction. The reporter can become a mini host for a quick game: a guess-the-category round, a two-minute mini-explanation of a strange phenomenon, or a rapid recap of the most surprising fact seen that day. The structure is loose, but the payoff is consistent: a shared memory that grows with each mile.

Beyond games, the reporter's notes are a practical bridge to the rest of your day. After you arrive at your destination, you can revisit the notes and turn them into short stories, a few lines in a family journal, or a quick recap for dinner time. You might tuck a few questions into your notes for later inquiry: what caused that weather pattern you saw by the highway, or how do certain inventions actually work in practice? You can let these questions simmer until you're back home, when a family research session becomes a new adventure and a reminder that learning isn't confined to school hours. The Power of this role is that it invites everyone to contribute to the family's map of curiosity. It's not about being right; it's about learning together, savoring the exchange, and building confidence in talking about ideas in front of others.

If you want a bit more structure without losing spontaneity, try a gentle routine. At the end of each day's ride, the reporter shares a favorite observation and a question to explore later. Then the family votes on which question feels most intriguing and assigns a light responsibility to someone to look it up or ponder it before the next trip. This keeps curiosity current and personal and gives every journey a narrative arc—the question, the investigation, the moment when the curiosity is fulfilled, and the next question that will carry you forward. The Road-Trip Reporter is not about producing perfect explanations. It's about cultivating a habit of curiosity that travels as freely as your car does, turning every window view into a prompt, every conversation into a mini-lesson, and every trip into a small, shared achievement.

Share the Fun

If the car is your stage, then the kitchen table, the living room floor, and the campsite are your backdrops for

Share the Fun. This section is about turning the facts you've gathered into moments that last longer than a ride and bring people together in laughter and wonder. Sharing is the natural extension of collecting; it converts curiosity into connection. The core idea is simple: celebrate the facts aloud, then invite others to react, remix, or challenge them with a game or a fresh angle. The moment you share, you invite conversation to take root, and conversation is the seedbed of memory. You are building a family culture where questions are welcomed, compliments are offered freely, and jokes are made without fear of misstep because the aim is delight, not perfection.

A central practice is to read a few cards aloud with enthusiasm, letting the rhythm of speech carry the joke or surprise. People respond with laughter, a chorus of astonishment, or a thoughtful pause. The goal is to keep the pace lively and inclusive so that even shy members feel invited to speak up. A natural companion to this is telling a short story that connects two or three cards. The stories don't need to be elaborate; a quick, vivid snapshot—of a whale that swims with a circus of barnacles, or a city that thrives on wind-powered streetlights—creates a bridge between disparate facts and a shared imagination. When a card sparks a story, you're doing more than sharing a fact—you're building a mythic map of your family's collective imagination and sense of humor.

Bedtime is a perfect stage for Share the Fun. As the house quiets, turn the day's discoveries into a gentle, entertaining ritual. Each person can pick a favorite card and retell it in their own voice, perhaps even giving it a punchline or a personal twist. The retellings become a family chorus, a harmless and endearing tradition that kids look forward to every night. If you have a child who loves improv, invite them to stretch a fact into a short, playful scene. If someone is more shy, offer a partner moment where they can co-read and share the starring role with a parent or sibling. The point is not to demand expert explanations but to celebrate the spark of curiosity and the joy of sharing that spark with others.

Another way to share is to transform facts into quick, light challenges. A fact can become the nucleus of a tiny quiz or a two-question game: guess the category, then guess the answer. These micro-games are low-stakes and high-reward, perfect for the car or the kitchen counter. You can also turn facts into jokes or silly puns, the kind of humor that travels well and sticks with people long after the moment has passed. The humor should be clean, gentle, and age-appropriate, ensuring that everyone in the car feels comfortable and included. The real magic of sharing lies in letting everyone see that learning can be funny, surprising, and personally meaningful, not just something that happens in a classroom. When laughter is part of the learning, curiosity becomes a friendly habit, something you reach for again and again without coaxing.

There's also value in collecting and sharing small stories that came from the shared fact pool. A card might remind someone of a family anecdote or a memory of a previous trip. Those connections turn mere trivia into memory artifacts—little souvenirs you can pull out when you want a smile. Over time, your family's book of discoveries grows into a living timeline of ideas, jokes, and questions that can be browsed, revisited, and added to. The goal of sharing isn't to crown a champion of trivia; it's to invite everyone into a circle where curiosity is valued, where questions are safe, and where the act of speaking up is celebrated. When sharing becomes part of how you wind down or relax after a trip, curiosity stops being something you do and becomes something you are as a family.

One Last 'Did You Know?' Challenge

The final section is a gentle, hopeful push toward making curiosity an everyday habit. The One Last Did You Know? Challenge is less a test and more a spark that travels from one trip to the next. The challenge is simple: end each ride by finding and sharing a new fact that surprised you today. It might be a small observation, a tiny detail you hadn't noticed before, or a larger idea you encountered in a story or a sign you passed. The point is to leave the car with a fresh nugget of wonder that can become a tasty morsel in the family's ongoing conversation. The rule is flexible and friendly: no repeats, no nitpicking, just one new spark to close out the trip. The simplicity is part of the magic because it lowers the barrier to participation and invites even the most reticent passenger to contribute.

To make the challenge feel like a ritual rather than a task, couple it with a quick, warm reflection. After you share the new fact, you can offer a short moment for everyone to say what that fact makes them wonder about or what it reminds them of. The goal is not to amass a database of trivia but to cultivate a shared sense of curiosity that you can carry into everyday life. A weekly ritual can help cement the habit: choose a night for a family curiosity wrap-up, where each person contributes their best new fact from the week and discusses any questions that arose from it. This creates a rhythm in which learning becomes a natural and welcome activity, not an occasional add-on.

If you keep a little notebook or a digital note beside your kitchen calendar, you can log the new facts you discovered on each trip. Over time, the notebook becomes more than a memory aid; it becomes a personal anthology of your family's curiosity. You'll notice patterns emerge—the kinds of questions that excite certain members, the topics that spark the most laughter, or the facts that lead to interesting offline scavenger hunts for future trips. You may even find that your trips begin to feel shorter as curiosity takes the place of restlessness. The act of seeking the new fact becomes the rhythm that carries you through the drive and through the day. The ultimate payoff is a sense of shared purpose: something you do together because it reminds you that the world is full of oddities worth noticing, worth discussing, and worth keeping alive as a family tradition. As you close each trip with a fresh fact, you give yourselves permission to keep exploring, to keep asking why, and to keep turning every mile into a laugh-out-loud, memory-making moment.

www.ingramcontent.com/pod-product-compliance
Lightning Source LLC
Chambersburg PA
CBHW071334080526
44587CB00017B/2838